The

CORE DISCIPLESHIP

Journal

THIS JOURNAL BELONGS TO

_____

ANCHOR CROSS
PUBLISHING

Anchor-Cross Publishing
P.O. Box 381682
Cambridge, MA 02238
www.anchorcross.org

ISBN 10: 0-9742727-7-1
ISBN 13: 978-0-9742727-7-1

This book is printed on acid-free paper.

INTRODUCTION

The Structure and Overarching Goal

Picture the Bible as a secure platform on a stormy sea. Humanity is thrashing about, looking for something solid, but grasping onto objects that are sinking. Only by finding the truth of the Scriptures can we stand secure. Like any platform, the Bible is not an end unto itself, but it enables us to know the true God and to become the people God wants us to be. Once we find our way onto this platform, we can meditate, pray, worship, fellowship, and rest. In short, the truth of God's word enables life. Without God's revelation, our knowledge of God would be amiss, impoverishing or tainting our thoughts, prayers, worship, words, and actions.

The journal you hold is premised on reading a portion of the Bible every day and using that passage as the basis of reflection, thanksgiving, repentance, application, prayer, and worship. We have found that a chapter a day works well for our family, but you could do more or less if that suits you. As a family, we choose a book of the Bible and work through that book in a chapter per day—every member of the family doing the same chapter each day—until we finish the book. Then we decide together which book to do next. We have not gone in any particularly strict sequence but have tried to balance across testaments and genres. In the past six months we have done, in order, Genesis, Acts, 1 John, Galatians, 1 Thessalonians,

Proverbs, Daniel, and Mark. For those who prefer, there are many Bible reading plans that you can find online to go through the Bible according to a predetermined schedule. We have intentionally kept this area flexible and not built the journal around a preset reading plan.

In the morning, we recommend doing the Bible reading, prayer, worship, and journaling. These activities should be done *alone*. We believe that every individual should daily engage in these spiritual disciplines alone with God. Then we recommend coming together as a family or group in the evening and sharing from your journal. That time of sharing forms the core of our household's family devotion time. Everyone contributes, and everyone learns from one another.

We strongly recommend using this journal as a married couple, family, or group of single people (such as a dorm or apartment). Even if you live alone, you could commit to doing this with other singles on your own and discussing what you've learned on a weekly basis. The four advantages of doing this together are consistent accountability, steady discipleship, synergistic learning, and relationship building.

Consistent accountability. Accountability is important for consistency. Naturally, reading the Bible and journaling as a group motivates you to be consistent. For most people, the structure that this journal offers will enable you to be consistent in the word and prayer, even if you have never been before! Of course, you could do this alone, but in our experience doing it with others makes it more likely that you will persist over the long run. This consistency will then develop into a lifelong habit. What better habits could one cultivate than daily time in the word, worship, and prayer, along with repentance, thanksgiving, and exhortation? It has been said that we make our habits and then our habits make us. These habits carry supernatural endowments of grace to change your life and the world.

Steady discipleship. Discipleship begins with prayer, reading the word, worship, confession, and gratitude (more on this later). Adopting the practices of this journal will sow the word of God into your hearts, facilitate consistent prayer, and draw you into worship. We have both found that this format has brought great gains into our discipleship. For more on this topic, watch the online message "Core discipleship comes through family worship" by Finny Kuruvilla.

Synergistic learning. We have seen that husbands are blessed and challenged to hear what their wives discovered in the identical passage that they read that morning. The reverse is also true. We both have been touched to hear what our children have learned. Because the entire family has read the same chapter in the morning, we can discuss the passage and what we learned in the car or over meals. Deuteronomy 6 says, "These words, which I command you today, shall be on your heart; and you shall teach them diligently to your children, and shall talk of them when you sit in your house, and when you walk by the way, and when you lie down, and when you rise up." Using this journal as a family or household and talking about what you have learned during the day will enable you to build a life in accordance with this pattern.

Relationship building. You will learn a great deal about the hearts of your spouse, children, siblings, or roommates as they share what they learned in this process. We believe that if done deliberately and patiently the topics of this journal will connect you to other's hearts in ways nothing else can. We advise not waiting until too late in the night when children might be tired (or you!) and allocating enough time so that you can truly listen to each other, ask questions, and discuss.

We want to be explicit about what this journal is not. This journal is not a productivity journal. Partly because of ever-increasing distraction, productivity journals have become very popular in recent years. While they have their place, we found it best to keep a dedicated and separate journal for Bible journaling and prayer.

The Components

Gratitude. Repentance. Regular Bible study. Faithful, persistent prayer. We all know that these are key practices to the Christian life, and yet many, many Christians struggle to make them a daily practice. This journal is meant to help you change all that. Each day, if you will show up, this journal will prompt you in each of these areas.

Gratitude. One of the most life-changing concepts is deceptively simple: "In everything give thanks, for this is the will of God in Christ Jesus toward you" (1 Thessalonians 5:18). Imagine a life where you **always** found something for which to give thanks. Even the secular world has grasped the necessity of gratitude; if we want to live a joyful life, we must live a grateful life. As Marcus Tullius Cicero wrote, "Gratitude is not only the greatest of virtues, but the parent of all the others." But as you have probably experienced, gratitude does not come naturally to most of us. It is easy to be grateful for a sunny Saturday with no work to do and no responsibilities to attend to; but the real test of gratitude comes on the rainy Monday morning, when the children are grumpy, or the boss is angry, or the traffic is snarled. And you have a headache. It is then that finding the gifts that God is giving in the moment will make the biggest difference. And so this journal acts as a tutor, reminding you each day, morning and evening, to look through the complicated web of your life and thank God for the beautiful gifts you find there.

Repentance. How could we best summarize Jesus' preaching in his three year ministry? "Repent, for the kingdom of God is at hand." A kingdom of righteousness is coming in victory to overtake the earth; repentance is the key that will make us ready to take part in that glorious kingdom. And while a thorough repentance is necessary to come to Jesus, a one-time act of repentance will not be enough. Repentance, like bread, must not be allowed to go stale; like bathing, it must be done again and again to keep us clean. A practice of daily repentance will keep us cleansed of our sin, ready to join our Savior and Maker in the glorious kingdom He is preparing. Thus this journal will remind you each evening to reflect on your day and repent of any wrong you have done.

Regular Bible study. Jesus said, "If you abide in my word, you are my disciples indeed. And you shall know the truth, and the truth shall make you free" (John 8:31). To abide is to dwell, to live within. How can we abide in the word of God if we do not ingest his written word daily? The word of God is the very truth, able to set us free— from sin, self, and Satan. Even for those committed to reading God's word daily, how easy is it to run your eyes over a passage without taking it in? We recommend using the following study questions to help (even, force!) you to go deeper in your understanding, even with the most familiar passages. The seven suggested questions are:

1. What does this passage say about God?

2. What does this passage say about the nature of humanity?

3. What truth can I find in this passage that propels me to worship God?

4. What promise(s) are found in this text? (Sometimes they may be implicit.) Try to identify a promise with relevance to your life or someone for whom you are praying.

5. Look at your own life: from this passage, is there something in my sinful nature that I can see more clearly and put to death?

6. What positive application can I make from this text?

7. Write out a prayer inspired by this passage.

These questions have been tested with children ten and over; with college freshmen; with adults who have been Christians for many years. We use them in our family worship. Each person over ten reads the same passage and answers the questions in private morning devotions; then in the evening, we share our responses at family worship. As we read through the Bible together, this practice has drawn us together; as we meditate on Scripture together, it has deepened our conversations and our corporate worship. Occasionally we deviate from these questions, but only rarely. We have been surprised at how these questions work across narratives (such as Genesis or Acts), epistles (such as 1 John or Galatians), poetry (such as Psalms or Proverbs), and even in chapters of genealogy! For some chapters, it is more difficult to find edifying answers to these questions, but the additional work will prove rewarding. "It is the glory of God to conceal a matter, it is the glory of kings to search it out" (Proverbs 25:2).

Prayer. The biblical story of the persistent widow is familiar enough: her persistent, unstopping pleas move the heart of an unjust judge. How much more will our loving Father hear our persistent prayers? And yet, how easy it is to give up after praying five times or twenty times for the same request, either from forgetfulness or from a weak-faithed assumption that God does not want to answer? In *The Circle Maker*, Mark Batterson gives modern examples of the persistent widow, with story after story of the rewards of persistent prayer. He describes the act of praying persistently as circling; as we pray we are like God's people in Jericho, circling round and round the city as we wait for the promised fall of the walls. Thus we have included here ten pages to write out prayer requests and the basis of those prayers, as well as numbers from 1-500 to circle in writing each time you circle them in prayer. We strongly recommend that you write out a basis for confidence in that prayer, whether it be a particular biblical promise, a providential event, or a leading of the Spirit. Most, if not all, of the great prayer warriors of the last two hundred years (John Hyde, George Muller, Hudson Taylor, Charles Finney) used prayer as a time to claim God's promises and understood prayer's power as bound up in an appeal to God's faithfulness.

Our prayer and hope is that this journal can be a faithful tutor to each of us, prompting us in these practices of faith and righteousness to help us grow up into the full image of our Savior.

Step-by-step

When you wake up in the morning, open your journal and locate today's Bible passage. Ask God to open your eyes and heart to the truth in His word, and begin reading with the questions in mind. Use the allotted space to answer the seven questions; sometimes it may be necessary to read the passage twice in order to answer each question. You can also use the blank lines to write out prayers inspired by the passage.

Another rich practice is to pray God's word back to Him, verse-by-verse. For example, consider Psalm 1:1-2, which speaks of the blessed person avoiding the paths of the wicked and the scoffer. Instead the righteous are those delighting in God's law and meditating on God's word day and night. You could pray, "May I avoid scoffing today. Forgive me for the times that I have spoken badly of others or been the negative cynic. Instead, may I delight in your word. May my heart be so captivated with your word that I speak of it to the people that I encounter today. And this verse speaks about meditating on your word day and night. You know that I struggle with wasting time at night. Help me instead to meditate on your word at night, and to delight in You." That is merely one possible direction. You could instead pray for more Bible translations so that more ethnic groups can read and delight in God's word. You could pray for your children by name that they would avoid the way of sinners and instead delight in God's word. The possibilities are vast. If you were reading Acts 1, you could begin by praying that you or a non-Christian friend or family member would see and believe the "infallible proofs" of His resurrection and come to understand the things Jesus spoke "pertaining to the kingdom of God" (Acts 1:3).

Praying the words of Scripture back to God is a powerful way to move out of the narrow path of your own mind and join in God's expansive, righteous view of the world and its events. These prayers facilitate reliance upon God's promises and His word. Many have found that praying verse-by-verse in a conversational manner breaks them out of the rut of short, perfunctory prayers.

Going down the page, you would next follow the prompt to worship God. You can start with your answer to question 3 (What reason can I find in this passage to worship God?) and turn that answer into active worship. Singing or praying through a psalm are other ways to begin your time of worship. Sometimes we will play a song from our phone or laptop to help draw us into worship as we sing along. (Of course, don't get distracted by some other task, like email or a website!) Often, as you worship God and pray the word, you will feel prompted in some way. Perhaps it is to call or visit someone and offer encouragement. Sometimes a word or promise is made real to your soul in a fresh way. Sometimes, your mind is drawn to a non-Christian friend or someone else that you should contact. Write these thoughts down! These moments of worship, reading the word, and prayer are the moments where you can best hear God. (For more on this, watch the message online by Finny Kuruvilla entitled "Hearing God's voice.") We have found this discipline of "Listening Prayer" to be especially sweet, tender, and life-changing.

Next, respond to the prompt to circle your prayers. Turn to the page where you've written these prayer requests; pray through each one, and circle the number to inspire you to keep persisting in prayer. Now, return to the day's page and respond to the final two questions, which will help you close out your time of prayer and worship. First, what can you be grateful for today? Try not to write the same thing day after day (family, food, etc), although our thanks for these things should be ongoing. At least, in addition to those daily thanks, look for something for which you can be particularly or uniquely grateful for today: yesterday's answered prayer; a beautiful sunrise shining through your window; a promise or glimpse into God's character that came home to you in a new way in the morning's Bible reading. The more specific, the better. Writing out thanks for your four-year old's smile and something she said is better than merely writing her name. Finally, pause to think of current situations that need your prayer today. These will probably be different from the prayers you already circled: a friend who is sick; a difficult situation you know you will face later in the day; a temptation that you battled yesterday and need victory from today.

At the close of your day, return to your journal to answer the two evening questions and again connect with your Maker. First, what do you need to confess from this day? What could you have done better? Keeping confession current is vital to abiding in communion with God. Thinking about what you could have done better is not an idle act of self-deprecation; writing out an answer will help you to remember your ideal response in a future similar situation. Next, the journal reminds you to thank God for specific events or provisions in your day. So often we forget to thank God for what He has done. Use this opportunity to give thanks in all circumstances, no matter whether the day was easy or difficult (1 Thess. 5:18). Finally, write out anything you want to remember from the day: a victory over sin; a special moment with a friend or family member; a noteworthy event. In this way, the journal will provide a valuable record of your days to look back on in the future.

A Sample Journal Entry

To help you in answering the questions, below are sample answers from journaling Acts 14.

1. <u>God</u> – God is the one working through his people when there is evangelistic success. (v. 27: "they reported all the things that God had done with them.")

2. <u>Humanity</u> – People tend to fit new occurrences into their own way of seeing the world—here, the assumption that Paul and Barnabas are Hermes and Zeus.

3. <u>Worship</u> – Worship God for always leaving a witness of Himself to all nations and generations through rain and fruitful seasons (v. 17). Nature itself testifies to His existence!

4. <u>Promise</u> – "Through many afflictions we must enter into God's kingdom" (v. 22) - but He will be with us through all the trials (Matthew 28:20). God kept His evangelists safe through incredible suffering. You will be with us when we share the good news.

5. <u>Put to Death</u> – Fear of offending or being thought strange for speaking about Jesus.

6. <u>Positive Application</u> – Notice how relentless Paul and the apostles were in preaching the gospel. Even after great physical and emotional suffering, they don't go on holiday. They persist by going to another city. I want to have this persistence in my life. I also want to study how Paul presents the gospels to those who have never studied the Bible (this chapter and Mars' Hill).

7. <u>Prayer</u> – Dear Father, Help me to be willing to speak to those I meet about you. Give me courage and wisdom to be sensitive for opportunities and to know what I should say.

After this, we would encourage you to journal from your "Listening prayer" time as you worship and pray.

A Final Note to Parents

Teach your children to develop the habit of a morning devotion with God. This habit is one of the best gifts that you can implant into their lives. Journaling will help them greatly in that practice. In our family, we ask that all children over the age of 10 engage in journaling. We have an eight-year old who does a portion of the questions, as she is able.

In the evening, we have found that doing our time of family devotions shortly after dinner is the best time, before the children become too tired. Make sure to allocate enough time that you do not feel rushed. And listen to their hearts and ask questions! The parents should lead out with confession and vulnerability, thus setting a tone for the whole family. In addition to sharing from the journal, we sing, memorize Scripture verses, and pray together. For our family of two parents and seven children (only six of whom can talk), we can do this well in about 30 minutes. When you encounter background topics that they may not be familiar with, stop and explain those topics. We've taught our children to draw out Paul's missionary journeys from memory and to understand the basic timeline and events of Scripture better. But of course, the best encouragement of all is to apply Scripture to our hearts and lives. We as parents are often thinking during the day about how to infuse our family devotion time with helpful instruction that would suit the passage and the circumstances that we then face.

May God bless you as you raise your children in the instruction of the Lord!

PRAYER REQUESTS

Prayer request #1

_____

_____

_____

_____

_____

_____

_____

_____

Basis of request (Promise from Scripture / Providential Event / Leading of the Spirit):

_____

_____

_____

_____

_____

_____

_____

_____

_____

_____

_____

_____

_____

_____

_____

_____

Circle your prayers

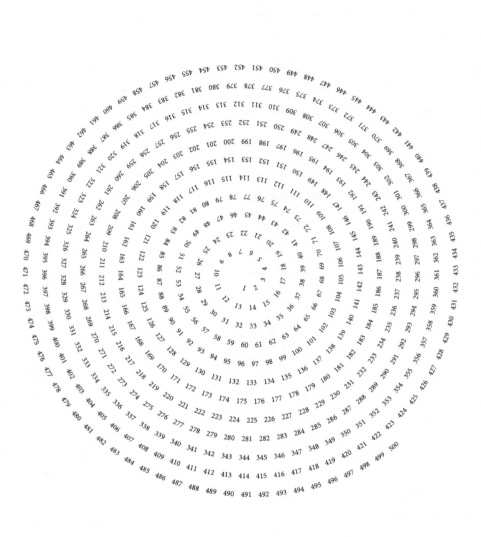

Prayer request #2

_____

_____

_____

_____

_____

_____

_____

_____

Basis of request (Promise from Scripture / Providential Event / Leading of the Spirit):

_____

_____

_____

_____

_____

_____

_____

_____

_____

_____

_____

_____

_____

_____

_____

_____

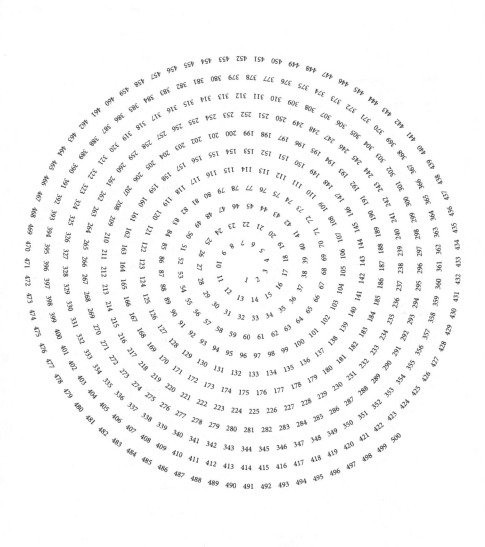

Prayer request #3

_____
_____
_____
_____
_____
_____
_____
_____
_____

Basis of request (Promise from Scripture / Providential Event / Leading of the Spirit):

_____
_____
_____
_____
_____
_____
_____
_____
_____
_____
_____
_____
_____
_____
_____
_____

Circle your prayers

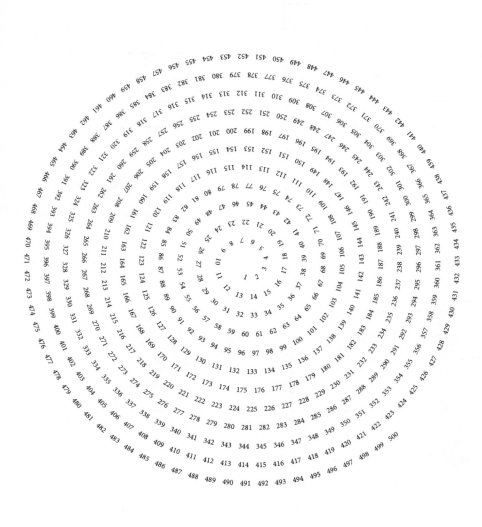

Prayer request #4

_____

_____

_____

_____

_____

_____

_____

_____

_____

Basis of request (Promise from Scripture / Providential Event / Leading of the Spirit):

_____

_____

_____

_____

_____

_____

_____

_____

_____

_____

_____

_____

_____

_____

_____

_____

Circle your prayers

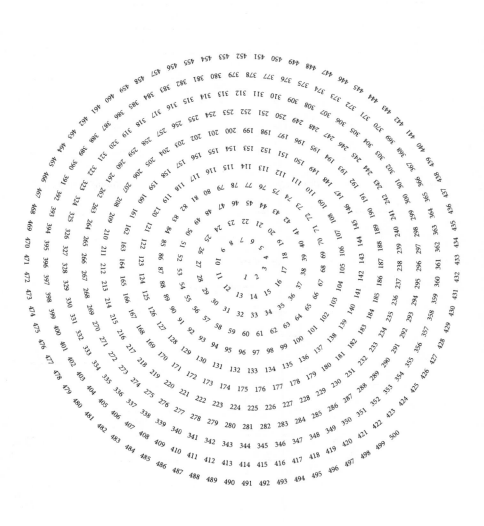

Prayer request #5

_____

_____

_____

_____

_____

_____

_____

_____

_____

Basis of request (Promise from Scripture / Providential Event / Leading of the Spirit):

_____

_____

_____

_____

_____

_____

_____

_____

_____

_____

_____

_____

_____

_____

_____

_____

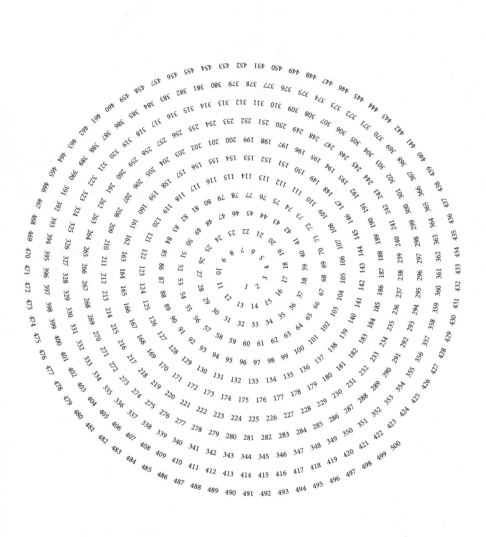

Prayer request #6

_____
_____
_____
_____
_____
_____
_____
_____
_____
_____

Basis of request (Promise from Scripture / Providential Event / Leading of the Spirit):

_____
_____
_____
_____
_____
_____
_____
_____
_____
_____
_____
_____
_____
_____
_____
_____
_____
_____
_____

Circle your prayers

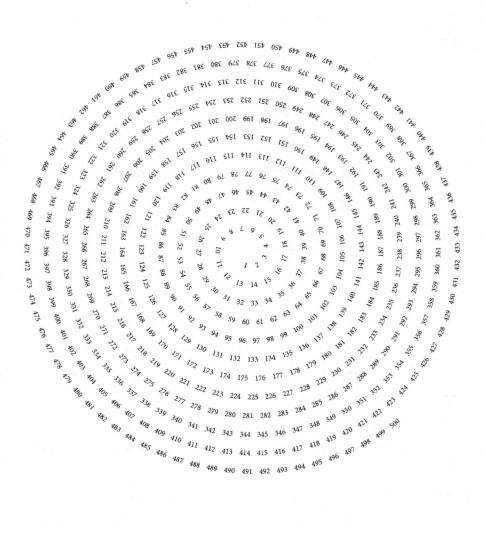

Prayer request #7

_____

_____

_____

_____

_____

_____

_____

_____

Basis of request (Promise from Scripture / Providential Event / Leading of the Spirit):

_____

_____

_____

_____

_____

_____

_____

_____

_____

_____

_____

_____

_____

_____

_____

Circle your prayers

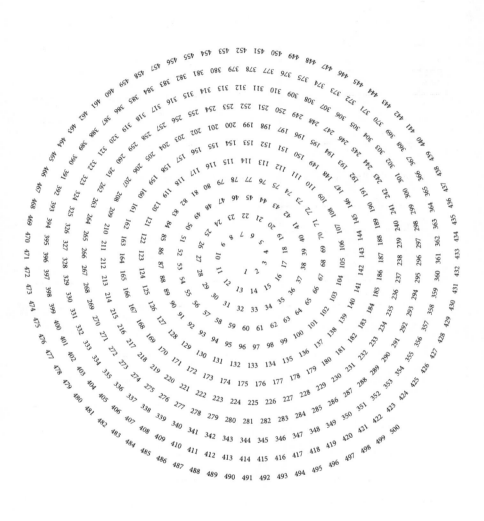

Prayer request #8

_____

_____

_____

_____

_____

_____

_____

_____

Basis of request (Promise from Scripture / Providential Event / Leading of the Spirit):

_____

_____

_____

_____

_____

_____

_____

_____

_____

_____

_____

_____

_____

_____

_____

_____

Circle your prayers

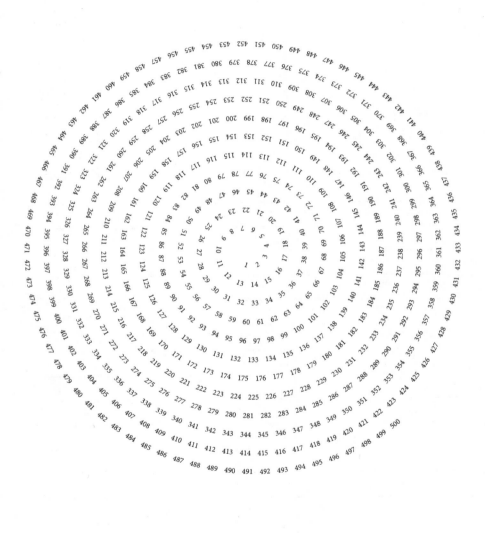

31

Prayer request #9

_____

_____

_____

_____

_____

_____

_____

_____

Basis of request (Promise from Scripture / Providential Event / Leading of the Spirit):

_____

_____

_____

_____

_____

_____

_____

_____

_____

_____

_____

_____

_____

_____

_____

_____

Circle your prayers

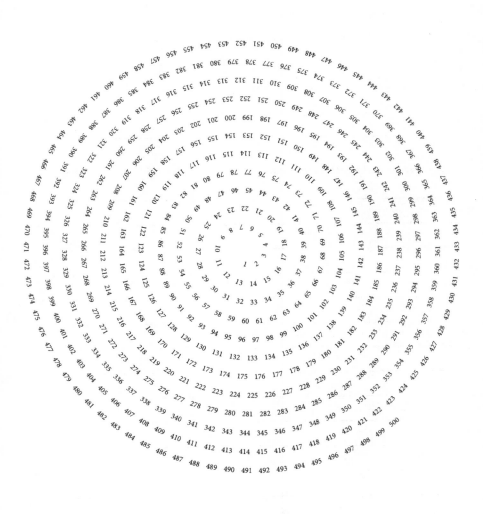

Prayer request #10

_____

_____

_____

_____

_____

_____

_____

_____

_____

Basis of request (Promise from Scripture / Providential Event / Leading of the Spirit):

_____

_____

_____

_____

_____

_____

_____

_____

_____

_____

_____

_____

_____

_____

_____

_____

Circle your prayers

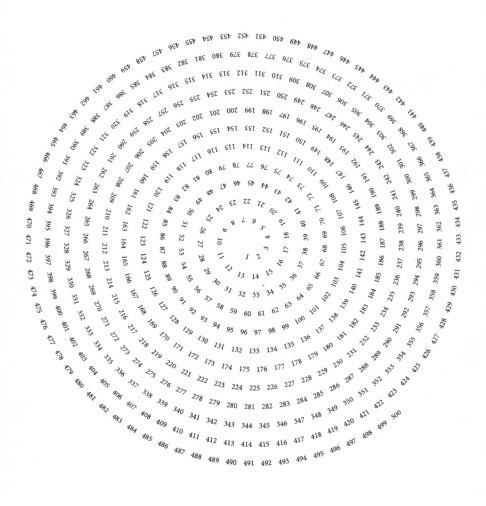

Extra Space for Prayers and Journaling

Daily Journal

"Praying without fervency is like hunting with a dead dog."

—CHARLES SPURGEON

DATE ____/____/____   TODAY'S BIBLE PASSAGE: _____

Reflections on the passage and prayer time

_____

_____

_____

_____

_____

_____

_____

_____

_____

_____

_____

_____

Time in worship ☐   *Time circling prayers* ☐   *Time in listening prayer* ☐

What can you thank God for this morning?

_____

_____

_____

What are important events or people to pray about today?

_____

_____

_____

_____

_____

_____

_____

_____

_____

_____

_____

_____

_____

_____

_____

_____

_____

_____

_____

_____

_____

_____

What sins would you like to confess? What could you have done better?

_____

_____

_____

For what would you like to thank God? What would you like to remember from today?

_____

_____

_____

> *"He is no fool who gives what he cannot keep to gain that which he cannot lose."*
>
> —Jim Elliot

DATE ____/____/____ TODAY'S BIBLE PASSAGE: _____

Reflections on the passage and prayer time

_____

_____

_____

_____

_____

_____

_____

_____

_____

_____

_____

_____

_____

Time in worship ☐   *Time circling prayers* ☐   *Time in listening prayer* ☐

What can you thank God for this morning?

_____

_____

_____

What are important events or people to pray about today?

_____

_____

_____

_____
_____
_____
_____
_____
_____
_____
_____
_____
_____
_____
_____
_____
_____
_____
_____
_____
_____
_____

What sins would you like to confess? What could you have done better?

_____
_____
_____

For what would you like to thank God? What would you like to remember from today?

_____
_____
_____

"Faith is like a lens. Properly arranged it will enable us to see things far off as if near."

—JOHN WYCLIFFE

DATE ____/____/____   TODAY'S BIBLE PASSAGE: _____

Reflections on the passage and prayer time

_____

_____

_____

_____

_____

_____

_____

_____

_____

_____

_____

_____

_____

Time in worship ☐   *Time circling prayers* ☐   *Time in listening prayer* ☐

What can you thank God for this morning?

_____

_____

_____

What are important events or people to pray about today?

_____

_____

_____

_____

_____

_____

_____

_____

_____

_____

_____

_____

_____

_____

_____

_____

_____

_____

_____

_____

_____

_____

_____

_____

_____

What sins would you like to confess? What could you have done better?

_____

_____

_____

For what would you like to thank God? What would you like to remember from today?

_____

_____

_____

> *"It is a safe thing to trust Him to fulfill the desires which He creates."*
>
> —AMY CARMICHAEL

DATE ____/____/____   TODAY'S BIBLE PASSAGE: _____

Reflections on the passage and prayer time

_____

_____

_____

_____

_____

_____

_____

_____

_____

_____

_____

_____

Time in worship ☐   *Time circling prayers* ☐   *Time in listening prayer* ☐

What can you thank God for this morning?

_____

_____

What are important events or people to pray about today?

_____

_____

_____

_____

_____

_____

_____

_____

_____

_____

_____

_____

_____

_____

_____

_____

_____

_____

_____

_____

_____

_____

_____

_____

What sins would you like to confess? What could you have done better?

_____

_____

_____

For what would you like to thank God? What would you like to remember from today?

_____

_____

_____

"To believe one does not need counsel is great pride."

—BASIL THE GREAT

DATE ____/____/____   TODAY'S BIBLE PASSAGE: _____

Reflections on the passage and prayer time

_____

_____

_____

_____

_____

_____

_____

_____

_____

_____

_____

_____

Time in worship ☐   *Time circling prayers* ☐   *Time in listening prayer* ☐

What can you thank God for this morning?

_____

_____

_____

What are important events or people to pray about today?

_____

_____

_____

_____

_____

_____

_____

_____

_____

_____

_____

_____

_____

_____

_____

_____

_____

_____

_____

_____

_____

_____

_____

_____

What sins would you like to confess? What could you have done better?

_____

_____

_____

For what would you like to thank God? What would you like to remember from today?

_____

_____

_____

"There are two kinds of people in the world—only two kinds. Not black or white, rich or poor, but those either dead in sin or dead to sin."

—LEONARD RAVENHILL

DATE ____/____/____   TODAY'S BIBLE PASSAGE: _____

Reflections on the passage and prayer time

_____
_____
_____
_____
_____
_____
_____
_____
_____
_____
_____
_____
_____

Time in worship ☐   *Time circling prayers* ☐   *Time in listening prayer* ☐

What can you thank God for this morning?

_____
_____
_____

What are important events or people to pray about today?

_____
_____
_____

_____
_____
_____
_____
_____
_____
_____
_____
_____
_____
_____
_____
_____
_____
_____
_____
_____
_____
_____
_____
_____

What sins would you like to confess? What could you have done better?

_____
_____
_____

For what would you like to thank God? What would you like to remember from today?

_____
_____
_____

> *"Unbelief is actually perverted faith, for it puts its trust not in the living God but in dying men."*
>
> **—A.W. Tozer**

DATE ____/____/____ TODAY'S BIBLE PASSAGE: _____

Reflections on the passage and prayer time

_____

_____

_____

_____

_____

_____

_____

_____

_____

_____

_____

_____

_____

Time in worship ☐   *Time circling prayers* ☐   *Time in listening prayer* ☐

What can you thank God for this morning?

_____

_____

_____

What are important events or people to pray about today?

_____

_____

_____

_____

_____

_____

_____

_____

_____

_____

_____

_____

_____

_____

_____

_____

_____

_____

_____

_____

_____

_____

What sins would you like to confess? What could you have done better?

_____

_____

_____

For what would you like to thank God? What would you like to remember from today?

_____

_____

_____

"Do not have your concert first, and then tune your instrument afterwards. Begin the day with the Word of God and prayer, and get first of all into harmony with Him."

—HUDSON TAYLOR

DATE ____/____/____ TODAY'S BIBLE PASSAGE: _____

Reflections on the passage and prayer time

_____

_____

_____

_____

_____

_____

_____

_____

_____

_____

_____

_____

Time in worship ☐ *Time circling prayers* ☐ *Time in listening prayer* ☐

What can you thank God for this morning?

_____

_____

_____

What are important events or people to pray about today?

_____

_____

_____

_____

_____

_____

_____

_____

_____

_____

_____

_____

_____

_____

_____

_____

_____

_____

_____

_____

_____

_____

_____

What sins would you like to confess? What could you have done better?

_____

_____

_____

For what would you like to thank God? What would you like to remember from today?

_____

_____

_____

"The waters are rising, but so am I. I am not going under, but over."
—CATHERINE BOOTH

DATE ____/____/____   TODAY'S BIBLE PASSAGE: _____

Reflections on the passage and prayer time

_____

_____

_____

_____

_____

_____

_____

_____

_____

_____

_____

_____

Time in worship ☐   *Time circling prayers* ☐   *Time in listening prayer* ☐

What can you thank God for this morning?

_____

_____

_____

What are important events or people to pray about today?

_____

_____

_____

_____

_____

_____

_____

_____

_____

_____

_____

_____

_____

_____

_____

_____

_____

_____

_____

_____

_____

_____

_____

_____

What sins would you like to confess? What could you have done better?

_____

_____

_____

For what would you like to thank God? What would you like to remember from today?

_____

_____

_____

"There's no greater lifestyle and no greater happiness than that of having a continual conversation with God."

—BROTHER LAWRENCE

DATE ____/____/____   TODAY'S BIBLE PASSAGE: _____

Reflections on the passage and prayer time

_____

_____

_____

_____

_____

_____

_____

_____

_____

_____

_____

_____

Time in worship ☐   *Time circling prayers* ☐   *Time in listening prayer* ☐

What can you thank God for this morning?

_____

_____

_____

What are important events or people to pray about today?

_____

_____

_____

_____

_____

_____

_____

_____

_____

_____

_____

_____

_____

_____

_____

_____

_____

_____

_____

_____

_____

_____

_____

What sins would you like to confess? What could you have done better?

_____

_____

_____

For what would you like to thank God? What would you like to remember from today?

_____

_____

_____

"I can plod. I can persevere in any definite pursuit.
To this I owe everything."

—WILLIAM CAREY

DATE ____/____/____   TODAY'S BIBLE PASSAGE: _____

Reflections on the passage and prayer time

_____

_____

_____

_____

_____

_____

_____

_____

_____

_____

_____

_____

Time in worship ☐   *Time circling prayers* ☐   *Time in listening prayer* ☐

What can you thank God for this morning?

_____

_____

_____

What are important events or people to pray about today?

_____

_____

_____

_____

_____

_____

_____

_____

_____

_____

_____

_____

_____

_____

_____

_____

_____

_____

_____

_____

_____

_____

_____

_____

What sins would you like to confess? What could you have done better?

_____

_____

_____

For what would you like to thank God? What would you like to remember from today?

_____

_____

_____

"Your accumulated offences do not surpass the multitude of God's mercies: your wounds do not surpass the Great Physician's skill."

—CYRIL OF JERUSALEM

DATE ____/____/____   TODAY'S BIBLE PASSAGE: _____

Reflections on the passage and prayer time

_____
_____
_____
_____
_____
_____
_____
_____
_____
_____
_____
_____

Time in worship ☐   *Time circling prayers* ☐   *Time in listening prayer* ☐

What can you thank God for this morning?

_____
_____
_____

What are important events or people to pray about today?

_____
_____
_____

_____

_____

_____

_____

_____

_____

_____

_____

_____

_____

_____

_____

_____

_____

_____

_____

_____

_____

_____

What sins would you like to confess? What could you have done better?

_____

_____

_____

For what would you like to thank God? What would you like to remember from today?

_____

_____

_____

"Temptation is like a knife, that may either cut the meat or the throat of a man; it may be his food or his poison, his exercise or his destruction."

—JOHN OWEN

DATE ____/____/____   TODAY'S BIBLE PASSAGE: _____

Reflections on the passage and prayer time

_____

_____

_____

_____

_____

_____

_____

_____

_____

_____

_____

_____

Time in worship ☐   *Time circling prayers* ☐   *Time in listening prayer* ☐

What can you thank God for this morning?

_____

_____

_____

What are important events or people to pray about today?

_____

_____

_____

_____

_____

_____

_____

_____

_____

_____

_____

_____

_____

_____

_____

_____

_____

_____

_____

_____

_____

_____

_____

What sins would you like to confess? What could you have done better?

_____

_____

_____

For what would you like to thank God? What would you like to remember from today?

_____

_____

_____

"God judges what we give by what we keep."
—GEORGE MULLER

DATE ____/____/____   TODAY'S BIBLE PASSAGE: _____

Reflections on the passage and prayer time

_____

_____

_____

_____

_____

_____

_____

_____

_____

_____

_____

_____

_____

Time in worship ☐   *Time circling prayers* ☐   *Time in listening prayer* ☐

What can you thank God for this morning?

_____

_____

_____

What are important events or people to pray about today?

_____

_____

_____

_____

_____

_____

_____

_____

_____

_____

_____

_____

_____

_____

_____

_____

_____

_____

_____

_____

_____

_____

_____

What sins would you like to confess? What could you have done better?

_____

_____

_____

For what would you like to thank God? What would you like to remember from today?

_____

_____

_____

"Pride must die in you, or nothing of heaven can live in you."
—ANDREW MURRAY

DATE ____/____/____   TODAY'S BIBLE PASSAGE: _____

Reflections on the passage and prayer time

_____
_____
_____
_____
_____
_____
_____
_____
_____
_____
_____
_____
_____

Time in worship ☐   *Time circling prayers* ☐   *Time in listening prayer* ☐

What can you thank God for this morning?

_____
_____
_____

What are important events or people to pray about today?

_____
_____
_____

What sins would you like to confess? What could you have done better?

For what would you like to thank God? What would you like to remember from today?

"As no darkness can be seen by anyone surrounded by light, so no trivialities can capture the attention of anyone who has his eyes on Christ."

—GREGORY OF NYSSA

DATE ____/____/____   TODAY'S BIBLE PASSAGE: _____

Reflections on the passage and prayer time

_____

_____

_____

_____

_____

_____

_____

_____

_____

_____

_____

_____

_____

Time in worship ☐   *Time circling prayers* ☐   *Time in listening prayer* ☐

What can you thank God for this morning?

_____

_____

_____

What are important events or people to pray about today?

_____

_____

_____

_____

_____

_____

_____

_____

_____

_____

_____

_____

_____

_____

_____

_____

_____

_____

_____

_____

_____

_____

_____

_____

What sins would you like to confess? What could you have done better?

_____

_____

_____

For what would you like to thank God? What would you like to remember from today?

_____

_____

_____

"Whatever you may do for your brother, being hungry, and a stranger, and naked, not even the devil will be able to despoil, but it will be laid up in an inviolable treasure."

—JOHN CHRYSOSTOM

DATE ____/____/____   TODAY'S BIBLE PASSAGE: _____

Reflections on the passage and prayer time

_____

_____

_____

_____

_____

_____

_____

_____

_____

_____

_____

_____

_____

Time in worship ☐   *Time circling prayers* ☐   *Time in listening prayer* ☐

What can you thank God for this morning?

_____

_____

_____

What are important events or people to pray about today?

_____

_____

_____

_____

_____

_____

_____

_____

_____

_____

_____

_____

_____

_____

_____

_____

_____

_____

_____

_____

_____

_____

_____

What sins would you like to confess? What could you have done better?

_____

_____

_____

For what would you like to thank God? What would you like to remember from today?

_____

_____

_____

"The tree of the promise will not drop its fruit unless shaken by the hand of prayer."

—THOMAS WATSON

DATE ____/____/____   TODAY'S BIBLE PASSAGE: _____

Reflections on the passage and prayer time

_____

_____

_____

_____

_____

_____

_____

_____

_____

_____

_____

_____

_____

_____

Time in worship ☐   *Time circling prayers* ☐   *Time in listening prayer* ☐

What can you thank God for this morning?

_____

_____

_____

What are important events or people to pray about today?

_____

_____

_____

_____

_____

_____

_____

_____

_____

_____

_____

_____

_____

_____

_____

_____

_____

_____

_____

_____

_____

_____

_____

What sins would you like to confess? What could you have done better?

_____

_____

_____

For what would you like to thank God? What would you like to remember from today?

_____

_____

_____

"You have not lived today until you have done something for someone who can never repay you."

—JOHN BUNYAN

DATE ____/____/____ TODAY'S BIBLE PASSAGE: _____

Reflections on the passage and prayer time

_____

_____

_____

_____

_____

_____

_____

_____

_____

_____

_____

_____

Time in worship ☐   *Time circling prayers* ☐   *Time in listening prayer* ☐

What can you thank God for this morning?

_____

_____

_____

What are important events or people to pray about today?

_____

_____

_____

_____

_____

_____

_____

_____

_____

_____

_____

_____

_____

_____

_____

_____

_____

_____

_____

_____

_____

_____

What sins would you like to confess? What could you have done better?

_____

_____

_____

For what would you like to thank God? What would you like to remember from today?

_____

_____

_____

"Expect great things from God! Attempt great things for God!"
—WILLIAM CAREY

DATE ____/____/____   TODAY'S BIBLE PASSAGE: _____

Reflections on the passage and prayer time

_____

_____

_____

_____

_____

_____

_____

_____

_____

_____

_____

_____

_____

Time in worship ☐   *Time circling prayers* ☐   *Time in listening prayer* ☐

What can you thank God for this morning?

_____

_____

_____

What are important events or people to pray about today?

_____

_____

_____

_____

_____

_____

_____

_____

_____

_____

_____

_____

_____

_____

_____

_____

_____

_____

_____

_____

_____

_____

_____

What sins would you like to confess? What could you have done better?

_____

_____

_____

For what would you like to thank God? What would you like to remember from today?

_____

_____

_____

"It is not that I want merely to be called a Christian, but actually to be one. Yes, if I prove to be one, then I can have the name."

—IGNATIUS OF ANTIOCH

DATE ____/____/____   TODAY'S BIBLE PASSAGE: _____

Reflections on the passage and prayer time

_____

_____

_____

_____

_____

_____

_____

_____

_____

_____

_____

_____

_____

Time in worship ☐   *Time circling prayers* ☐   *Time in listening prayer* ☐

What can you thank God for this morning?

_____

_____

_____

What are important events or people to pray about today?

_____

_____

_____

What sins would you like to confess? What could you have done better?

For what would you like to thank God? What would you like to remember from today?

> *"God sends no one away empty except those who are full of themselves."*
>
> —DWIGHT L. MOODY

DATE ____/____/____   TODAY'S BIBLE PASSAGE: _____

Reflections on the passage and prayer time

_____

_____

_____

_____

_____

_____

_____

_____

_____

_____

_____

_____

_____

Time in worship ☐   *Time circling prayers* ☐   *Time in listening prayer* ☐

What can you thank God for this morning?

_____

_____

_____

What are important events or people to pray about today?

_____

_____

_____

_____

_____

_____

_____

_____

_____

_____

_____

_____

_____

_____

_____

_____

_____

_____

_____

_____

What sins would you like to confess? What could you have done better?

_____

_____

_____

For what would you like to thank God? What would you like to remember from today?

_____

_____

_____

*"Worrying is carrying tomorrow's load with today's strength—
carrying two days at once. It is moving into tomorrow ahead of time."*

—CORRIE TEN BOOM

DATE ____/____/____   TODAY'S BIBLE PASSAGE: _____

Reflections on the passage and prayer time

_____

_____

_____

_____

_____

_____

_____

_____

_____

_____

_____

_____

Time in worship ☐   *Time circling prayers* ☐   *Time in listening prayer* ☐

What can you thank God for this morning?

_____

_____

_____

What are important events or people to pray about today?

_____

_____

_____

_____

_____

_____

_____

_____

_____

_____

_____

_____

_____

_____

_____

_____

_____

_____

_____

_____

_____

_____

_____

_____

_____

What sins would you like to confess? What could you have done better?

_____

_____

_____

For what would you like to thank God? What would you like to remember from today?

_____

_____

_____

"The early church was married to poverty, prisons and persecutions. Today, the church is married to prosperity, personality, and popularity."

— LEONARD RAVENHILL

DATE ____/____/____   TODAY'S BIBLE PASSAGE: _____

Reflections on the passage and prayer time

_____

_____

_____

_____

_____

_____

_____

_____

_____

_____

_____

_____

Time in worship ☐   *Time circling prayers* ☐   *Time in listening prayer* ☐

What can you thank God for this morning?

_____

_____

_____

What are important events or people to pray about today?

_____

_____

_____

_____

_____

_____

_____

_____

_____

_____

_____

_____

_____

_____

_____

_____

_____

_____

_____

_____

_____

_____

What sins would you like to confess? What could you have done better?

_____

_____

_____

For what would you like to thank God? What would you like to remember from today?

_____

_____

_____

"It is always possible to be thankful for what is given rather than to com-plain about what is not given. One or the other becomes a habit of life."

—ELISABETH ELLIOT

DATE ____/____/____   TODAY'S BIBLE PASSAGE: _____

Reflections on the passage and prayer time

_____

_____

_____

_____

_____

_____

_____

_____

_____

_____

_____

_____

_____

Time in worship ☐   *Time circling prayers* ☐   *Time in listening prayer* ☐

What can you thank God for this morning?

_____

_____

_____

What are important events or people to pray about today?

_____

_____

_____

_____

_____

_____

_____

_____

_____

_____

_____

_____

_____

_____

_____

_____

_____

_____

_____

_____

_____

_____

What sins would you like to confess? What could you have done better?

_____

_____

_____

For what would you like to thank God? What would you like to remember from today?

_____

_____

_____

"Men try to cheat themselves into the belief that sin is not quite so sinful as God says it is, and that they are not so bad as they really are."

—J.C. RYLE

DATE ____/____/____   TODAY'S BIBLE PASSAGE: _____

Reflections on the passage and prayer time

_____

_____

_____

_____

_____

_____

_____

_____

_____

_____

_____

_____

_____

Time in worship ☐   *Time circling prayers* ☐   *Time in listening prayer* ☐

What can you thank God for this morning?

_____

_____

_____

What are important events or people to pray about today?

_____

_____

_____

_____

_____

_____

_____

_____

_____

_____

_____

_____

_____

_____

_____

_____

_____

_____

_____

_____

_____

_____

What sins would you like to confess? What could you have done better?

_____

_____

_____

For what would you like to thank God? What would you like to remember from today?

_____

_____

_____

"Be killing sin or it will be killing you."
—John Owen

DATE ____/____/____   TODAY'S BIBLE PASSAGE: _____

Reflections on the passage and prayer time

_____

_____

_____

_____

_____

_____

_____

_____

_____

_____

_____

_____

Time in worship ☐   *Time circling prayers* ☐   *Time in listening prayer* ☐

What can you thank God for this morning?

_____

_____

_____

What are important events or people to pray about today?

_____

_____

_____

_____
_____
_____
_____
_____
_____
_____
_____
_____
_____
_____
_____
_____
_____
_____
_____
_____
_____
_____

What sins would you like to confess? What could you have done better?

_____
_____
_____

For what would you like to thank God? What would you like to remember from today?

_____
_____
_____

> *"The story of every great Christian achievement is the history of answered prayer."*
>
> —E. M. Bounds

DATE ____/____/____   TODAY'S BIBLE PASSAGE: _____

Reflections on the passage and prayer time

_____

_____

_____

_____

_____

_____

_____

_____

_____

_____

_____

Time in worship ☐   *Time circling prayers* ☐   *Time in listening prayer* ☐

What can you thank God for this morning?

_____

_____

_____

What are important events or people to pray about today?

_____

_____

_____

_____

_____

_____

_____

_____

_____

_____

_____

_____

_____

_____

_____

_____

_____

_____

_____

_____

_____

What sins would you like to confess? What could you have done better?

_____

_____

_____

For what would you like to thank God? What would you like to remember from today?

_____

_____

_____

"I have a great need for Christ; I have a great Christ for my need."
—CHARLES SPURGEON

DATE ____/____/____   TODAY'S BIBLE PASSAGE: _____

Reflections on the passage and prayer time

_____

_____

_____

_____

_____

_____

_____

_____

_____

_____

_____

_____

_____

Time in worship ☐   *Time circling prayers* ☐   *Time in listening prayer* ☐

What can you thank God for this morning?

_____

_____

_____

What are important events or people to pray about today?

_____

_____

_____

_____

_____

_____

_____

_____

_____

_____

_____

_____

_____

_____

_____

_____

_____

_____

_____

_____

_____

_____

What sins would you like to confess? What could you have done better?

_____

_____

_____

For what would you like to thank God? What would you like to remember from today?

_____

_____

_____

"God's work done in God's way will never lack God's supply."
—HUDSON TAYLOR

DATE ____/____/____   TODAY'S BIBLE PASSAGE: _____

Reflections on the passage and prayer time

_____

_____

_____

_____

_____

_____

_____

_____

_____

_____

_____

_____

_____

Time in worship ☐   *Time circling prayers* ☐   *Time in listening prayer* ☐

What can you thank God for this morning?

_____

_____

_____

What are important events or people to pray about today?

_____

_____

_____

_____

_____

_____

_____

_____

_____

_____

_____

_____

_____

_____

_____

_____

_____

_____

_____

_____

_____

_____

_____

_____

What sins would you like to confess? What could you have done better?

_____

_____

_____

For what would you like to thank God? What would you like to remember from today?

_____

_____

_____

*"Effective prayer is often like the felling of a great tree—
it takes repeated blows."*

—JOHN ELDREDGE

DATE ____/____/____ TODAY'S BIBLE PASSAGE: _____

Reflections on the passage and prayer time

_____

_____

_____

_____

_____

_____

_____

_____

_____

_____

_____

_____

Time in worship ☐   *Time circling prayers* ☐   *Time in listening prayer* ☐

What can you thank God for this morning?

_____

_____

_____

What are important events or people to pray about today?

_____

_____

_____

_____

_____

_____

_____

_____

_____

_____

_____

_____

_____

_____

_____

_____

_____

_____

_____

_____

_____

_____

_____

What sins would you like to confess? What could you have done better?

_____

_____

_____

For what would you like to thank God? What would you like to remember from today?

_____

_____

_____

"If a commission by an earthly king is considered a honor, how can a commission by a Heavenly King be considered a sacrifice?"

—DAVID LIVINGSTONE

DATE ____/____/____   TODAY'S BIBLE PASSAGE: _____

Reflections on the passage and prayer time

_____

_____

_____

_____

_____

_____

_____

_____

_____

_____

_____

Time in worship ☐   *Time circling prayers* ☐   *Time in listening prayer* ☐

What can you thank God for this morning?

_____

_____

What are important events or people to pray about today?

_____

_____

_____

_____

_____

_____

_____

_____

_____

_____

_____

_____

_____

_____

_____

_____

_____

_____

_____

_____

_____

_____

What sins would you like to confess? What could you have done better?

_____

_____

_____

For what would you like to thank God? What would you like to remember from today?

_____

_____

_____

"If we are willing to put ourselves into God's hands, then God is willing to use us. But there are two conditions: obedience and purity."

—JOHN HYDE

DATE ____/____/____ TODAY'S BIBLE PASSAGE: _____

Reflections on the passage and prayer time

_____

_____

_____

_____

_____

_____

_____

_____

_____

_____

_____

_____

Time in worship ☐   *Time circling prayers* ☐   *Time in listening prayer* ☐

What can you thank God for this morning?

_____

_____

_____

What are important events or people to pray about today?

_____

_____

_____

_____

_____

_____

_____

_____

_____

_____

_____

_____

_____

_____

_____

_____

_____

_____

_____

_____

_____

_____

_____

What sins would you like to confess? What could you have done better?

_____

_____

_____

For what would you like to thank God? What would you like to remember from today?

_____

_____

_____

> *"That God is good is taught or implied on every page of the Bible and must be received as an article of faith as impregnable as the throne of God."*
>
> —A.W. TOZER

DATE ____/____/____ TODAY'S BIBLE PASSAGE: _____

Reflections on the passage and prayer time

_____
_____
_____
_____
_____
_____
_____
_____
_____
_____
_____
_____
_____

Time in worship ☐   *Time circling prayers* ☐   *Time in listening prayer* ☐

What can you thank God for this morning?

_____
_____
_____

What are important events or people to pray about today?

_____
_____
_____

_____

_____

_____

_____

_____

_____

_____

_____

_____

_____

_____

_____

_____

_____

_____

_____

_____

_____

_____

What sins would you like to confess? What could you have done better?

_____

_____

_____

For what would you like to thank God? What would you like to remember from today?

_____

_____

_____

*"God has two thrones—the one in the highest heavens,
the other in the lowliest hearts."*

—UNKNOWN

DATE ____/____/____   TODAY'S BIBLE PASSAGE: _____

Reflections on the passage and prayer time

_____

_____

_____

_____

_____

_____

_____

_____

_____

_____

_____

_____

Time in worship ☐   *Time circling prayers* ☐   *Time in listening prayer* ☐

What can you thank God for this morning?

_____

_____

_____

What are important events or people to pray about today?

_____

_____

_____

_____
_____
_____
_____
_____
_____
_____
_____
_____
_____
_____
_____
_____
_____
_____
_____
_____
_____
_____

What sins would you like to confess? What could you have done better?

_____
_____
_____

For what would you like to thank God? What would you like to remember from today?

_____
_____
_____

"You can give without loving. But you cannot love without giving."
—AMY CARMICHAEL

DATE ____/____/____   TODAY'S BIBLE PASSAGE: _____

Reflections on the passage and prayer time

_____
_____
_____
_____
_____
_____
_____
_____
_____
_____
_____
_____
_____

Time in worship ☐   *Time circling prayers* ☐   *Time in listening prayer* ☐

What can you thank God for this morning?

_____
_____
_____

What are important events or people to pray about today?

_____
_____
_____

_____

_____

_____

_____

_____

_____

_____

_____

_____

_____

_____

_____

_____

_____

_____

_____

_____

_____

_____

What sins would you like to confess? What could you have done better?

_____

_____

_____

For what would you like to thank God? What would you like to remember from today?

_____

_____

_____

"People who do not know the Lord ask why in the world we waste our lives as missionaries. They forget that they too are expending their lives ... and when the bubble has burst, they will have nothing of eternal significance to show for the years they have wasted."
—NATE SAINT

DATE ____/____/____   TODAY'S BIBLE PASSAGE: _____

Reflections on the passage and prayer time

_____

_____

_____

_____

_____

_____

_____

_____

_____

_____

_____

_____

_____

Time in worship ☐   *Time circling prayers* ☐   *Time in listening prayer* ☐

What can you thank God for this morning?

_____

_____

_____

What are important events or people to pray about today?

_____

_____

_____

_____

_____

_____

_____

_____

_____

_____

_____

_____

_____

_____

_____

_____

_____

_____

_____

_____

_____

_____

_____

What sins would you like to confess? What could you have done better?

_____

_____

_____

For what would you like to thank God? What would you like to remember from today?

_____

_____

_____

"When there's something in the Bible that churches don't like, they call it legalism."

—LEONARD RAVENHILL

DATE ____/____/____   TODAY'S BIBLE PASSAGE: _____

Reflections on the passage and prayer time

_____
_____
_____
_____
_____
_____
_____
_____
_____
_____
_____
_____
_____

Time in worship ☐   *Time circling prayers* ☐   *Time in listening prayer* ☐

What can you thank God for this morning?

_____
_____
_____

What are important events or people to pray about today?

_____
_____
_____

_____

_____

_____

_____

_____

_____

_____

_____

_____

_____

_____

_____

_____

_____

_____

_____

_____

_____

_____

_____

_____

What sins would you like to confess? What could you have done better?

_____

_____

_____

For what would you like to thank God? What would you like to remember from today?

_____

_____

_____

"The great thing in prayer is to feel that we are putting our supplications into the bosom of omnipotent love."

—ANDREW MURRAY

DATE ____/____/____ TODAY'S BIBLE PASSAGE: _____

Reflections on the passage and prayer time

_____

_____

_____

_____

_____

_____

_____

_____

_____

_____

_____

_____

_____

Time in worship ☐   *Time circling prayers* ☐   *Time in listening prayer* ☐

What can you thank God for this morning?

_____

_____

_____

What are important events or people to pray about today?

_____

_____

_____

_____

_____

_____

_____

_____

_____

_____

_____

_____

_____

_____

_____

_____

_____

_____

_____

_____

_____

_____

What sins would you like to confess? What could you have done better?

_____

_____

_____

For what would you like to thank God? What would you like to remember from today?

_____

_____

_____

"The Christian ideal has not been tried and found wanting.
It has been found difficult; and left untried."

—G.K. CHESTERTON

DATE ____/____/____   TODAY'S BIBLE PASSAGE: _____

Reflections on the passage and prayer time

_____

_____

_____

_____

_____

_____

_____

_____

_____

_____

_____

_____

_____

_____

Time in worship ☐   *Time circling prayers* ☐   *Time in listening prayer* ☐

What can you thank God for this morning?

_____

_____

_____

What are important events or people to pray about today?

_____

_____

_____

_____

_____

_____

_____

_____

_____

_____

_____

_____

_____

_____

_____

_____

_____

_____

_____

_____

_____

_____

_____

What sins would you like to confess? What could you have done better?

_____

_____

_____

For what would you like to thank God? What would you like to remember from today?

_____

_____

_____

*"Forgiveness is setting the prisoner free, only to find out
that the prisoner was me."*

—CORRIE TEN BOOM

DATE ____/____/____   TODAY'S BIBLE PASSAGE: _____

Reflections on the passage and prayer time

_____

_____

_____

_____

_____

_____

_____

_____

_____

_____

_____

_____

_____

Time in worship ☐   *Time circling prayers* ☐   *Time in listening prayer* ☐

What can you thank God for this morning?

_____

_____

_____

What are important events or people to pray about today?

_____

_____

_____

What sins would you like to confess? What could you have done better?

For what would you like to thank God? What would you like to remember from today?

> *"God loves importunate prayer so much that He will not give us much blessing without it."*
>
> —ADONIRAM JUDSON

DATE ____/____/____ TODAY'S BIBLE PASSAGE: _____

Reflections on the passage and prayer time

_____

_____

_____

_____

_____

_____

_____

_____

_____

_____

_____

_____

Time in worship ☐   *Time circling prayers* ☐   *Time in listening prayer* ☐

What can you thank God for this morning?

_____

_____

What are important events or people to pray about today?

_____

_____

_____

_____

_____

_____

_____

_____

_____

_____

_____

_____

_____

_____

_____

_____

_____

_____

_____

_____

_____

_____

_____

_____

What sins would you like to confess? What could you have done better?

_____

_____

_____

For what would you like to thank God? What would you like to remember from today?

_____

_____

_____

"There are three great truths, 1st, That there is a God; 2nd, That He has spoken to us in the Bible; 3rd, That He means what He says."

—HUDSON TAYLOR

DATE ____/____/____   TODAY'S BIBLE PASSAGE: _____

Reflections on the passage and prayer time

_____

_____

_____

_____

_____

_____

_____

_____

_____

_____

_____

_____

_____

Time in worship ☐   *Time circling prayers* ☐   *Time in listening prayer* ☐

What can you thank God for this morning?

_____

_____

_____

What are important events or people to pray about today?

_____

_____

_____

_____

_____

_____

_____

_____

_____

_____

_____

_____

_____

_____

_____

_____

_____

_____

_____

_____

_____

_____

_____

What sins would you like to confess? What could you have done better?

_____

_____

_____

For what would you like to thank God? What would you like to remember from today?

_____

_____

_____

"In prayer it is better to have a heart without words than words without a heart."

—JOHN BUNYAN

DATE ____/____/____ TODAY'S BIBLE PASSAGE: _____

Reflections on the passage and prayer time

_____

_____

_____

_____

_____

_____

_____

_____

_____

_____

_____

Time in worship ☐   *Time circling prayers* ☐   *Time in listening prayer* ☐

What can you thank God for this morning?

_____

_____

_____

What are important events or people to pray about today?

_____

_____

_____

_____

_____

_____

_____

_____

_____

_____

_____

_____

_____

_____

_____

_____

_____

_____

_____

_____

_____

_____

_____

What sins would you like to confess? What could you have done better?

_____

_____

_____

For what would you like to thank God? What would you like to remember from today?

_____

_____

_____

> *"The business of the Christian is nothing else than*
> *to be ever preparing for death."*
> —IRENAEUS

DATE ____/____/____   TODAY'S BIBLE PASSAGE: _____

Reflections on the passage and prayer time

_____

_____

_____

_____

_____

_____

_____

_____

_____

_____

_____

_____

_____

Time in worship ☐   *Time circling prayers* ☐   *Time in listening prayer* ☐

What can you thank God for this morning?

_____

_____

_____

What are important events or people to pray about today?

_____

_____

_____

_____

_____

_____

_____

_____

_____

_____

_____

_____

_____

_____

_____

_____

_____

_____

_____

_____

_____

_____

What sins would you like to confess? What could you have done better?

_____

_____

_____

For what would you like to thank God? What would you like to remember from today?

_____

_____

_____

"To be little with God is to be little for God."

—EM BOUNDS

DATE ____/____/____ TODAY'S BIBLE PASSAGE: _____

Reflections on the passage and prayer time

_____

_____

_____

_____

_____

_____

_____

_____

_____

_____

_____

_____

_____

Time in worship ☐   *Time circling prayers* ☐   *Time in listening prayer* ☐

What can you thank God for this morning?

_____

_____

_____

What are important events or people to pray about today?

_____

_____

_____

_____

_____

_____

_____

_____

_____

_____

_____

_____

_____

_____

_____

_____

_____

_____

_____

_____

_____

What sins would you like to confess? What could you have done better?

_____

_____

_____

For what would you like to thank God? What would you like to remember from today?

_____

_____

_____

"Why will God's creatures sin against His throne? Can there be such madness in beings gifted with reason's light?"

—CHARLES FINNEY

DATE ____/____/____　TODAY'S BIBLE PASSAGE: _____

Reflections on the passage and prayer time

_____

_____

_____

_____

_____

_____

_____

_____

_____

_____

_____

_____

Time in worship ☐　*Time circling prayers* ☐　*Time in listening prayer* ☐

What can you thank God for this morning?

_____

_____

_____

What are important events or people to pray about today?

_____

_____

_____

_____
_____
_____
_____
_____
_____
_____
_____
_____
_____
_____
_____
_____
_____
_____
_____
_____
_____
_____
_____

What sins would you like to confess? What could you have done better?

_____
_____
_____

For what would you like to thank God? What would you like to remember from today?

_____
_____
_____

> *"Prayer is my real business! Cobbling shoes is a sideline; it just helps me pay expenses."*
>
> **—WILLIAM CAREY**

DATE ____/____/____   TODAY'S BIBLE PASSAGE: _____

Reflections on the passage and prayer time

_____

_____

_____

_____

_____

_____

_____

_____

_____

_____

_____

_____

Time in worship ☐   *Time circling prayers* ☐   *Time in listening prayer* ☐

What can you thank God for this morning?

_____

_____

_____

What are important events or people to pray about today?

_____

_____

_____

What sins would you like to confess? What could you have done better?

For what would you like to thank God? What would you like to remember from today?

*"Interceding produces better dividends
than criticizing or complaining."*

—DEREK PRINCE

DATE ____/____/____   TODAY'S BIBLE PASSAGE: _____

Reflections on the passage and prayer time

_____

_____

_____

_____

_____

_____

_____

_____

_____

_____

_____

_____

_____

Time in worship ☐   *Time circling prayers* ☐   *Time in listening prayer* ☐

What can you thank God for this morning?

_____

_____

_____

What are important events or people to pray about today?

_____

_____

_____

_____

_____

_____

_____

_____

_____

_____

_____

_____

_____

_____

_____

_____

_____

_____

_____

_____

_____

_____

_____

What sins would you like to confess? What could you have done better?

_____

_____

_____

For what would you like to thank God? What would you like to remember from today?

_____

_____

_____

"If I take offence easily; if I am content to continue in cold unfriendliness, though friendship be possible, then I know nothing of Calvary love."

—AMY CARMICHAEL

DATE ____/____/____   TODAY'S BIBLE PASSAGE: _____

Reflections on the passage and prayer time

_____

_____

_____

_____

_____

_____

_____

_____

_____

_____

_____

_____

Time in worship ☐   *Time circling prayers* ☐   *Time in listening prayer* ☐

What can you thank God for this morning?

_____

_____

_____

What are important events or people to pray about today?

_____

_____

_____

_____

_____

_____

_____

_____

_____

_____

_____

_____

_____

_____

_____

_____

_____

_____

_____

_____

_____

_____

What sins would you like to confess? What could you have done better?

_____

_____

_____

For what would you like to thank God? What would you like to remember from today?

_____

_____

_____

"You can do more than pray, after you have prayed, but you can never do more than pray until you have prayed."

—AJ GORDON

DATE ____/____/____   TODAY'S BIBLE PASSAGE: _____

Reflections on the passage and prayer time

_____

_____

_____

_____

_____

_____

_____

_____

_____

_____

_____

_____

_____

Time in worship ☐   *Time circling prayers* ☐   *Time in listening prayer* ☐

What can you thank God for this morning?

_____

_____

_____

What are important events or people to pray about today?

_____

_____

_____

_____

_____

_____

_____

_____

_____

_____

_____

_____

_____

_____

_____

_____

_____

_____

_____

_____

_____

_____

What sins would you like to confess? What could you have done better?

_____

_____

_____

For what would you like to thank God? What would you like to remember from today?

_____

_____

_____

> *"A Bible that's falling apart usually belongs to someone who isn't."*
> —CHARLES SPURGEON

DATE ____/____/____   TODAY'S BIBLE PASSAGE: _____

Reflections on the passage and prayer time

_____
_____
_____
_____
_____
_____
_____
_____
_____
_____
_____
_____
_____

Time in worship ☐   *Time circling prayers* ☐   *Time in listening prayer* ☐

What can you thank God for this morning?

_____
_____
_____

What are important events or people to pray about today?

_____
_____
_____

_____

_____

_____

_____

_____

_____

_____

_____

_____

_____

_____

_____

_____

_____

_____

_____

_____

_____

_____

_____

What sins would you like to confess? What could you have done better?

_____

_____

_____

For what would you like to thank God? What would you like to remember from today?

_____

_____

_____

"One of these days some simple soul will pick up the book of God, read it, and believe it. Then the rest of us will be embarrassed."

—LEONARD RAVENHILL

DATE ___/___/___ TODAY'S BIBLE PASSAGE: _____

Reflections on the passage and prayer time

_____

_____

_____

_____

_____

_____

_____

_____

_____

_____

_____

_____

_____

Time in worship ☐   *Time circling prayers* ☐   *Time in listening prayer* ☐

What can you thank God for this morning?

_____

_____

_____

What are important events or people to pray about today?

_____

_____

_____

_____

_____

_____

_____

_____

_____

_____

_____

_____

_____

_____

_____

_____

_____

_____

_____

_____

_____

_____

_____

_____

What sins would you like to confess? What could you have done better?

_____

_____

_____

For what would you like to thank God? What would you like to remember from today?

_____

_____

_____

"Faith does not operate in the realm of the possible.
There is no glory for God in that which is humanly possible.
Faith begins where man's power ends."
—GEORGE MULLER

DATE ____/____/____ TODAY'S BIBLE PASSAGE: _____

Reflections on the passage and prayer time

_____

_____

_____

_____

_____

_____

_____

_____

_____

_____

_____

_____

_____

Time in worship ☐   *Time circling prayers* ☐   *Time in listening prayer* ☐

What can you thank God for this morning?

_____

_____

_____

What are important events or people to pray about today?

_____

_____

_____

_____

_____

_____

_____

_____

_____

_____

_____

_____

_____

_____

_____

_____

_____

_____

_____

_____

_____

What sins would you like to confess? What could you have done better?

_____

_____

_____

For what would you like to thank God? What would you like to remember from today?

_____

_____

_____

> *"It is of the nature of love that it cannot lie quiescent."*
> **—A.W. Tozer**

DATE ____/____/____   TODAY'S BIBLE PASSAGE: _____

Reflections on the passage and prayer time

_____

_____

_____

_____

_____

_____

_____

_____

_____

_____

_____

_____

Time in worship ☐   *Time circling prayers* ☐   *Time in listening prayer* ☐

What can you thank God for this morning?

_____

_____

_____

What are important events or people to pray about today?

_____

_____

_____

_____
_____
_____
_____
_____
_____
_____
_____
_____
_____
_____
_____
_____
_____
_____
_____
_____
_____
_____
_____
_____

What sins would you like to confess? What could you have done better?

_____
_____
_____

For what would you like to thank God? What would you like to remember from today?

_____
_____
_____

"The difference between true and false repentance lies in this: the man who truly repents cries out against his heart; but the other, as Eve, against the serpent, or something else."

—JOHN BUNYAN

DATE ____/____/____   TODAY'S BIBLE PASSAGE: _____

Reflections on the passage and prayer time

_____

_____

_____

_____

_____

_____

_____

_____

_____

_____

_____

_____

_____

Time in worship ☐   *Time circling prayers* ☐   *Time in listening prayer* ☐

What can you thank God for this morning?

_____

_____

_____

What are important events or people to pray about today?

_____

_____

_____

_____

_____

_____

_____

_____

_____

_____

_____

_____

_____

_____

_____

_____

_____

_____

_____

_____

_____

What sins would you like to confess? What could you have done better?

_____

_____

_____

For what would you like to thank God? What would you like to remember from today?

_____

_____

_____

*"You will know as much of God, and only as much of God,
as you are willing to put into practice."*

—ERIC LIDDELL

DATE ____/____/____   TODAY'S BIBLE PASSAGE: _____

Reflections on the passage and prayer time

_____

_____

_____

_____

_____

_____

_____

_____

_____

_____

_____

_____

_____

Time in worship ☐   *Time circling prayers* ☐   *Time in listening prayer* ☐

What can you thank God for this morning?

_____

_____

_____

What are important events or people to pray about today?

_____

_____

_____

_____

_____

_____

_____

_____

_____

_____

_____

_____

_____

_____

_____

_____

_____

_____

_____

_____

_____

_____

_____

What sins would you like to confess? What could you have done better?

_____

_____

_____

For what would you like to thank God? What would you like to remember from today?

_____

_____

_____

"This surely is a good rule: whenever you see a fault in any other man, or any other church, look for it in yourself and in your own church."

—PHILIPS BROOKS

DATE ____/____/____   TODAY'S BIBLE PASSAGE: _____

Reflections on the passage and prayer time

_____

_____

_____

_____

_____

_____

_____

_____

_____

_____

_____

_____

_____

Time in worship ☐   *Time circling prayers* ☐   *Time in listening prayer* ☐

What can you thank God for this morning?

_____

_____

_____

What are important events or people to pray about today?

_____

_____

_____

_____

_____

_____

_____

_____

_____

_____

_____

_____

_____

_____

_____

_____

_____

_____

_____

_____

_____

_____

_____

_____

What sins would you like to confess? What could you have done better?

_____

_____

_____

For what would you like to thank God? What would you like to remember from today?

_____

_____

_____

"All God's giants have been weak men and women who have gotten hold of God's faithfulness."

—HUDSON TAYLOR

DATE ____/____/____ TODAY'S BIBLE PASSAGE: _____

Reflections on the passage and prayer time

_____

_____

_____

_____

_____

_____

_____

_____

_____

_____

_____

_____

_____

Time in worship ☐   *Time circling prayers* ☐   *Time in listening prayer* ☐

What can you thank God for this morning?

_____

_____

_____

What are important events or people to pray about today?

_____

_____

_____

_____
_____
_____
_____
_____
_____
_____
_____
_____
_____
_____
_____
_____
_____
_____
_____
_____
_____
_____
_____

What sins would you like to confess? What could you have done better?

_____
_____
_____

For what would you like to thank God? What would you like to remember from today?

_____
_____
_____

"Intimate knowledge of God is possible if we habitually search His Holy Scriptures & translate what we find into obedience."

—GEORGE MULLER

DATE ____/____/____   TODAY'S BIBLE PASSAGE: _____

Reflections on the passage and prayer time

_____

_____

_____

_____

_____

_____

_____

_____

_____

_____

_____

_____

_____

Time in worship ☐   *Time circling prayers* ☐   *Time in listening prayer* ☐

What can you thank God for this morning?

_____

_____

_____

What are important events or people to pray about today?

_____

_____

_____

_____

_____

_____

_____

_____

_____

_____

_____

_____

_____

_____

_____

_____

_____

_____

_____

_____

_____

_____

What sins would you like to confess? What could you have done better?

_____

_____

_____

For what would you like to thank God? What would you like to remember from today?

_____

_____

_____

*"If any man thinks ill of you, do not be angry with him,
for you are worse than he thinks you to be."*

—CHARLES SPURGEON

DATE ____/____/____ TODAY'S BIBLE PASSAGE: _____

Reflections on the passage and prayer time

_____
_____
_____
_____
_____
_____
_____
_____
_____
_____
_____
_____
_____

Time in worship ☐   *Time circling prayers* ☐   *Time in listening prayer* ☐

What can you thank God for this morning?

_____
_____
_____

What are important events or people to pray about today?

_____
_____
_____

_____
_____
_____
_____
_____
_____
_____
_____
_____
_____
_____
_____
_____
_____
_____
_____
_____
_____
_____
_____

What sins would you like to confess? What could you have done better?

_____
_____
_____

For what would you like to thank God? What would you like to remember from today?

_____
_____
_____

"If my life is fruitless, it doesn't matter who praises me, and if my life is fruitful, it doesn't matter who criticizes me."

—JOHN BUNYAN

DATE ____/____/____   TODAY'S BIBLE PASSAGE: _____

Reflections on the passage and prayer time

_____

_____

_____

_____

_____

_____

_____

_____

_____

_____

_____

_____

Time in worship ☐   *Time circling prayers* ☐   *Time in listening prayer* ☐

What can you thank God for this morning?

_____

_____

_____

What are important events or people to pray about today?

_____

_____

_____

_____
_____
_____
_____
_____
_____
_____
_____
_____
_____
_____
_____
_____
_____
_____
_____
_____
_____
_____
_____
_____
_____

What sins would you like to confess? What could you have done better?

_____
_____
_____

For what would you like to thank God? What would you like to remember from today?

_____
_____
_____

"As often, therefore, as you are asked for aid, believe that you are tried by God, that it may be seen whether you are worthy of being heard."

—LACTANTIUS

DATE ____/____/____   TODAY'S BIBLE PASSAGE: _____

Reflections on the passage and prayer time

_____

_____

_____

_____

_____

_____

_____

_____

_____

_____

_____

_____

Time in worship ☐   *Time circling prayers* ☐   *Time in listening prayer* ☐

What can you thank God for this morning?

_____

_____

What are important events or people to pray about today?

_____

_____

_____

What sins would you like to confess? What could you have done better?

For what would you like to thank God? What would you like to remember from today?

"To this end, man's duty is to learn the will of God, and to trustingly do that will, leaving results and events with God."

—DAVID LIPSCOMB

DATE ____/____/____ TODAY'S BIBLE PASSAGE: _____

Reflections on the passage and prayer time

_____

_____

_____

_____

_____

_____

_____

_____

_____

_____

_____

_____

Time in worship ☐   *Time circling prayers* ☐   *Time in listening prayer* ☐

What can you thank God for this morning?

_____

_____

_____

What are important events or people to pray about today?

_____

_____

_____

_____

_____

_____

_____

_____

_____

_____

_____

_____

_____

_____

_____

_____

_____

_____

_____

_____

_____

_____

_____

What sins would you like to confess? What could you have done better?

_____

_____

_____

For what would you like to thank God? What would you like to remember from today?

_____

_____

_____

"If Jesus Christ be God and died for me, then no sacrifice can be too great for me to make for Him."

—C.T. STUDD

DATE ____/____/____ TODAY'S BIBLE PASSAGE: _____

Reflections on the passage and prayer time

_____

_____

_____

_____

_____

_____

_____

_____

_____

_____

_____

_____

Time in worship ☐   *Time circling prayers* ☐   *Time in listening prayer* ☐

What can you thank God for this morning?

_____

_____

_____

What are important events or people to pray about today?

_____

_____

_____

_____

_____

_____

_____

_____

_____

_____

_____

_____

_____

_____

_____

_____

_____

_____

_____

_____

_____

_____

_____

What sins would you like to confess? What could you have done better?

_____

_____

_____

For what would you like to thank God? What would you like to remember from today?

_____

_____

_____

"Entertainment is the devil's substitute for joy. The more joy you have in the Lord the less entertainment you need."

—LEONARD RAVENHILL

DATE ____/____/____   TODAY'S BIBLE PASSAGE: _____

Reflections on the passage and prayer time

_____

_____

_____

_____

_____

_____

_____

_____

_____

_____

_____

_____

_____

_____

_____

Time in worship ☐   *Time circling prayers* ☐   *Time in listening prayer* ☐

What can you thank God for this morning?

_____

_____

_____

What are important events or people to pray about today?

_____

_____

_____

_____

_____

_____

_____

_____

_____

_____

_____

_____

_____

_____

_____

_____

_____

_____

_____

_____

_____

_____

_____

_____

_____

What sins would you like to confess? What could you have done better?

_____

_____

_____

For what would you like to thank God? What would you like to remember from today?

_____

_____

_____

"The secret is Christ in me, not me in a different set of circumstances."

—ELISABETH ELLIOT

DATE ____/____/____   TODAY'S BIBLE PASSAGE: _____

Reflections on the passage and prayer time

_____

_____

_____

_____

_____

_____

_____

_____

_____

_____

_____

Time in worship ☐   *Time circling prayers* ☐   *Time in listening prayer* ☐

What can you thank God for this morning?

_____

_____

_____

What are important events or people to pray about today?

_____

_____

_____

_____
_____
_____
_____
_____
_____
_____
_____
_____
_____
_____
_____
_____
_____
_____
_____
_____
_____
_____

What sins would you like to confess? What could you have done better?

_____
_____
_____

For what would you like to thank God? What would you like to remember from today?

_____
_____
_____

"The Bible is a promise book and a prayer book ...
Reading is the way you get through the Bible;
prayer is the way you get the Bible through you."
—MARK BATTERSON

DATE ____/____/____   TODAY'S BIBLE PASSAGE: _____

Reflections on the passage and prayer time

_____

_____

_____

_____

_____

_____

_____

_____

_____

_____

_____

_____

Time in worship ☐   *Time circling prayers* ☐   *Time in listening prayer* ☐

What can you thank God for this morning?

_____

_____

_____

What are important events or people to pray about today?

_____

_____

_____

_____

_____

_____

_____

_____

_____

_____

_____

_____

_____

_____

_____

_____

_____

_____

_____

_____

_____

_____

_____

_____

_____

What sins would you like to confess? What could you have done better?

_____

_____

_____

For what would you like to thank God? What would you like to remember from today?

_____

_____

_____

"When we work, we work. When we pray, God works."
—HUDSON TAYLOR

DATE ____/____/____   TODAY'S BIBLE PASSAGE: _____

Reflections on the passage and prayer time

_____

_____

_____

_____

_____

_____

_____

_____

_____

_____

_____

_____

_____

_____

Time in worship ☐   *Time circling prayers* ☐   *Time in listening prayer* ☐

What can you thank God for this morning?

_____

_____

_____

What are important events or people to pray about today?

_____

_____

_____

_____

_____

_____

_____

_____

_____

_____

_____

_____

_____

_____

_____

_____

_____

_____

_____

_____

_____

What sins would you like to confess? What could you have done better?

_____

_____

_____

For what would you like to thank God? What would you like to remember from today?

_____

_____

_____

> *"Pray and read, read and pray; for a little from God is better than a great deal from men."*
>
> —JOHN BUNYAN

DATE ____/____/____ TODAY'S BIBLE PASSAGE: _____

Reflections on the passage and prayer time

_____
_____
_____
_____
_____
_____
_____
_____
_____
_____
_____
_____
_____

Time in worship ☐   *Time circling prayers* ☐   *Time in listening prayer* ☐

What can you thank God for this morning?

_____
_____
_____

What are important events or people to pray about today?

_____
_____
_____

_____

_____

_____

_____

_____

_____

_____

_____

_____

_____

_____

_____

_____

_____

_____

_____

_____

_____

_____

_____

_____

_____

What sins would you like to confess? What could you have done better?

_____

_____

_____

For what would you like to thank God? What would you like to remember from today?

_____

_____

_____

> *"We say we are too busy to pray.*
> *But the busier our Lord was, the more He prayed."*
>
> —THE KNEELING CHRISTIAN

DATE ____/____/____   TODAY'S BIBLE PASSAGE: _____

Reflections on the passage and prayer time

_____

_____

_____

_____

_____

_____

_____

_____

_____

_____

_____

_____

Time in worship ☐   *Time circling prayers* ☐   *Time in listening prayer* ☐

What can you thank God for this morning?

_____

_____

_____

What are important events or people to pray about today?

_____

_____

_____

_____
_____
_____
_____
_____
_____
_____
_____
_____
_____
_____
_____
_____
_____
_____
_____
_____
_____
_____

What sins would you like to confess? What could you have done better?

_____
_____
_____

For what would you like to thank God? What would you like to remember from today?

_____
_____
_____

"All along, let us remember we are not asked to understand, but simply to obey."

—AMY CARMICHAEL

DATE ____/____/____ TODAY'S BIBLE PASSAGE: _____

Reflections on the passage and prayer time

_____

_____

_____

_____

_____

_____

_____

_____

_____

_____

_____

_____

Time in worship ☐   *Time circling prayers* ☐   *Time in listening prayer* ☐

What can you thank God for this morning?

_____

_____

_____

What are important events or people to pray about today?

_____

_____

_____

_____

_____

_____

_____

_____

_____

_____

_____

_____

_____

_____

_____

_____

_____

_____

_____

_____

What sins would you like to confess? What could you have done better?

_____

_____

_____

For what would you like to thank God? What would you like to remember from today?

_____

_____

_____

*"Even if we stand at the very summit of virtue,
it is by mercy that we shall be saved."*

—JOHN CHRYSOSTOM

DATE ____/____/____   TODAY'S BIBLE PASSAGE: _____

Reflections on the passage and prayer time

_____

_____

_____

_____

_____

_____

_____

_____

_____

_____

_____

_____

_____

Time in worship ☐   *Time circling prayers* ☐   *Time in listening prayer* ☐

What can you thank God for this morning?

_____

_____

_____

What are important events or people to pray about today?

_____

_____

_____

What sins would you like to confess? What could you have done better?

For what would you like to thank God? What would you like to remember from today?

"Questioning someone's salvation could possibly be one of the most loving things you can do for another."

—DEAN INSERRA

DATE ____/____/____   TODAY'S BIBLE PASSAGE: _____

Reflections on the passage and prayer time

_____

_____

_____

_____

_____

_____

_____

_____

_____

_____

_____

_____

Time in worship ☐   *Time circling prayers* ☐   *Time in listening prayer* ☐

What can you thank God for this morning?

_____

_____

_____

What are important events or people to pray about today?

_____

_____

_____

_____

_____

_____

_____

_____

_____

_____

_____

_____

_____

_____

_____

_____

_____

_____

_____

_____

_____

_____

_____

What sins would you like to confess? What could you have done better?

_____

_____

_____

For what would you like to thank God? What would you like to remember from today?

_____

_____

_____

"God's purpose in redemption is to make worshipers out of rebels."
—A.W. TOZER

DATE ____/____/____   TODAY'S BIBLE PASSAGE: _____

Reflections on the passage and prayer time

_____

_____

_____

_____

_____

_____

_____

_____

_____

_____

_____

_____

_____

Time in worship ☐   *Time circling prayers* ☐   *Time in listening prayer* ☐

What can you thank God for this morning?

_____

_____

_____

What are important events or people to pray about today?

_____

_____

_____

_____

_____

_____

_____

_____

_____

_____

_____

_____

_____

_____

_____

_____

_____

_____

_____

_____

_____

_____

What sins would you like to confess? What could you have done better?

_____

_____

_____

For what would you like to thank God? What would you like to remember from today?

_____

_____

_____

"Prayer is not supplemental—it is instrumental."
—Unknown

DATE ____/____/____   TODAY'S BIBLE PASSAGE: _____

Reflections on the passage and prayer time

_____
_____
_____
_____
_____
_____
_____
_____
_____
_____
_____
_____

Time in worship ☐   *Time circling prayers* ☐   *Time in listening prayer* ☐

What can you thank God for this morning?

_____
_____
_____

What are important events or people to pray about today?

_____
_____
_____

_____

_____

_____

_____

_____

_____

_____

_____

_____

_____

_____

_____

_____

_____

_____

_____

_____

_____

_____

What sins would you like to confess? What could you have done better?

_____

_____

_____

For what would you like to thank God? What would you like to remember from today?

_____

_____

_____

"There is no pit so deep, that God's love is not deeper still."
—CORRIE TEN BOOM

DATE ____/____/____   TODAY'S BIBLE PASSAGE: _____

Reflections on the passage and prayer time

_____

_____

_____

_____

_____

_____

_____

_____

_____

_____

_____

_____

_____

Time in worship ☐   *Time circling prayers* ☐   *Time in listening prayer* ☐

What can you thank God for this morning?

_____

_____

_____

What are important events or people to pray about today?

_____

_____

_____

_____

_____

_____

_____

_____

_____

_____

_____

_____

_____

_____

_____

_____

_____

_____

_____

_____

_____

_____

What sins would you like to confess? What could you have done better?

_____

_____

_____

For what would you like to thank God? What would you like to remember from today?

_____

_____

_____

"The truths that I know best I have learned on my knees. I never know a thing well, till it is burned into my heart by prayer."

—John Bunyan

DATE ____/____/____   TODAY'S BIBLE PASSAGE: _____

Reflections on the passage and prayer time

_____
_____
_____
_____
_____
_____
_____
_____
_____
_____
_____
_____
_____

Time in worship ☐   *Time circling prayers* ☐   *Time in listening prayer* ☐

What can you thank God for this morning?

_____
_____

What are important events or people to pray about today?

_____
_____
_____

_____

_____

_____

_____

_____

_____

_____

_____

_____

_____

_____

_____

_____

_____

_____

_____

_____

_____

What sins would you like to confess? What could you have done better?

_____

_____

_____

For what would you like to thank God? What would you like to remember from today?

_____

_____

_____

"Humility, the place of entire dependence on God, is the first duty and the highest virtue of the creature, and the root of every virtue."

—ANDREW MURRAY

DATE ____/____/____ TODAY'S BIBLE PASSAGE: _____

Reflections on the passage and prayer time

_____

_____

_____

_____

_____

_____

_____

_____

_____

_____

_____

_____

_____

Time in worship ☐   *Time circling prayers* ☐   *Time in listening prayer* ☐

What can you thank God for this morning?

_____

_____

_____

What are important events or people to pray about today?

_____

_____

_____

_____

_____

_____

_____

_____

_____

_____

_____

_____

_____

_____

_____

_____

_____

_____

_____

_____

_____

_____

What sins would you like to confess? What could you have done better?

_____

_____

_____

For what would you like to thank God? What would you like to remember from today?

_____

_____

_____

"Merely having an open mind is nothing. The object of opening the mind, as of opening the mouth, is to shut it again on something solid."

—G. K. CHESTERSTON

DATE ____/____/____   TODAY'S BIBLE PASSAGE: _____

Reflections on the passage and prayer time

_____

_____

_____

_____

_____

_____

_____

_____

_____

_____

_____

_____

_____

Time in worship ☐   *Time circling prayers* ☐   *Time in listening prayer* ☐

What can you thank God for this morning?

_____

_____

_____

What are important events or people to pray about today?

_____

_____

_____

_____

_____

_____

_____

_____

_____

_____

_____

_____

_____

_____

_____

_____

_____

_____

_____

_____

_____

_____

_____

What sins would you like to confess? What could you have done better?

_____

_____

_____

For what would you like to thank God? What would you like to remember from today?

_____

_____

_____

*"I believe the word of God without a complicated interpretation,
and out of this belief I speak."*

—CONRAD GREBEL

DATE ____/____/____   TODAY'S BIBLE PASSAGE: _____

Reflections on the passage and prayer time

_____

_____

_____

_____

_____

_____

_____

_____

_____

_____

_____

_____

Time in worship ☐   *Time circling prayers* ☐   *Time in listening prayer* ☐

What can you thank God for this morning?

_____

_____

_____

What are important events or people to pray about today?

_____

_____

_____

_____

_____

_____

_____

_____

_____

_____

_____

_____

_____

_____

_____

_____

_____

_____

_____

_____

_____

_____

_____

What sins would you like to confess? What could you have done better?

_____

_____

_____

For what would you like to thank God? What would you like to remember from today?

_____

_____

_____

"You can judge the quality of their faith from the way they behave. Discipline is an index to doctrine."

—TERTULLIAN

DATE ____/____/____   TODAY'S BIBLE PASSAGE: _____

Reflections on the passage and prayer time

_____

_____

_____

_____

_____

_____

_____

_____

_____

_____

_____

_____

_____

Time in worship ☐   *Time circling prayers* ☐   *Time in listening prayer* ☐

What can you thank God for this morning?

_____

_____

_____

What are important events or people to pray about today?

_____

_____

_____

_____

_____

_____

_____

_____

_____

_____

_____

_____

_____

_____

_____

_____

_____

_____

_____

_____

_____

What sins would you like to confess? What could you have done better?

_____

_____

_____

For what would you like to thank God? What would you like to remember from today?

_____

_____

_____

"Is the world crucified to you or does it fascinate you?"
—LEONARD RAVENHILL

DATE ____/____/____   TODAY'S BIBLE PASSAGE: _____

Reflections on the passage and prayer time

_____

_____

_____

_____

_____

_____

_____

_____

_____

_____

_____

_____

_____

Time in worship ☐   *Time circling prayers* ☐   *Time in listening prayer* ☐

What can you thank God for this morning?

_____

_____

_____

What are important events or people to pray about today?

_____

_____

_____

_____

_____

_____

_____

_____

_____

_____

_____

_____

_____

_____

_____

_____

_____

_____

_____

_____

_____

_____

_____

What sins would you like to confess? What could you have done better?

_____

_____

_____

For what would you like to thank God? What would you like to remember from today?

_____

_____

_____

"Grace is not opposed to effort, it is opposed to earning."
—DALLAS WILLARD

DATE ____/____/____ TODAY'S BIBLE PASSAGE: _____

Reflections on the passage and prayer time

_____

_____

_____

_____

_____

_____

_____

_____

_____

_____

_____

_____

Time in worship ☐   *Time circling prayers* ☐   *Time in listening prayer* ☐

What can you thank God for this morning?

_____

_____

_____

What are important events or people to pray about today?

_____

_____

_____

_____

_____

_____

_____

_____

_____

_____

_____

_____

_____

_____

_____

_____

_____

_____

_____

_____

_____

_____

_____

What sins would you like to confess? What could you have done better?

_____

_____

_____

For what would you like to thank God? What would you like to remember from today?

_____

_____

_____

"Prayer is the pulse of the renewed soul; and the constancy of its beat is the test and measure of the spiritual life."

—OCTAVIUS WINSLOW

DATE ____/____/____ TODAY'S BIBLE PASSAGE: _____

Reflections on the passage and prayer time

_____
_____
_____
_____
_____
_____
_____
_____
_____
_____
_____
_____
_____

Time in worship ☐ *Time circling prayers* ☐ *Time in listening prayer* ☐

What can you thank God for this morning?

_____
_____
_____

What are important events or people to pray about today?

_____
_____
_____

_____

_____

_____

_____

_____

_____

_____

_____

_____

_____

_____

_____

_____

_____

_____

_____

_____

_____

_____

_____

_____

_____

What sins would you like to confess? What could you have done better?

_____

_____

_____

For what would you like to thank God? What would you like to remember from today?

_____

_____

_____

> *"One single soul saved shall outlive and outweigh
> all the kingdoms of the world."*
>
> —J.C. RYLE

DATE ____/____/____   TODAY'S BIBLE PASSAGE: _____

Reflections on the passage and prayer time

_____
_____
_____
_____
_____
_____
_____
_____
_____
_____
_____
_____
_____

Time in worship ☐   *Time circling prayers* ☐   *Time in listening prayer* ☐

What can you thank God for this morning?

_____
_____
_____

What are important events or people to pray about today?

_____
_____
_____

_____

_____

_____

_____

_____

_____

_____

_____

_____

_____

_____

_____

_____

_____

_____

_____

_____

_____

_____

What sins would you like to confess? What could you have done better?

_____

_____

_____

For what would you like to thank God? What would you like to remember from today?

_____

_____

_____

"Remember that thought is speech before God."

—CHARLES SPURGEON

DATE ____/____/____   TODAY'S BIBLE PASSAGE: _____

Reflections on the passage and prayer time

_____

_____

_____

_____

_____

_____

_____

_____

_____

_____

_____

_____

_____

Time in worship ☐   *Time circling prayers* ☐   *Time in listening prayer* ☐

What can you thank God for this morning?

_____

_____

_____

What are important events or people to pray about today?

_____

_____

_____

_____

_____

_____

_____

_____

_____

_____

_____

_____

_____

_____

_____

_____

_____

_____

_____

_____

_____

_____

What sins would you like to confess? What could you have done better?

_____

_____

_____

For what would you like to thank God? What would you like to remember from today?

_____

_____

_____

> *"The old self-sins must die, and the only instrument*
> *by which they can be slain is the Cross."*
>
> —A.W. TOZER

DATE ____/____/____   TODAY'S BIBLE PASSAGE: _____

Reflections on the passage and prayer time

_____

_____

_____

_____

_____

_____

_____

_____

_____

_____

_____

_____

_____

Time in worship ☐   *Time circling prayers* ☐   *Time in listening prayer* ☐

What can you thank God for this morning?

_____

_____

_____

What are important events or people to pray about today?

_____

_____

_____

_____
_____
_____
_____
_____
_____
_____
_____
_____
_____
_____
_____
_____
_____
_____
_____
_____
_____

What sins would you like to confess? What could you have done better?

_____
_____
_____

For what would you like to thank God? What would you like to remember from today?

_____
_____
_____

> *"What God says is best, is best, though all the men*
> *in the world are against it."*
>
> —JOHN BUNYAN

DATE ____/____/____   TODAY'S BIBLE PASSAGE: _____

Reflections on the passage and prayer time

_____

_____

_____

_____

_____

_____

_____

_____

_____

_____

_____

_____

_____

Time in worship ☐   *Time circling prayers* ☐   *Time in listening prayer* ☐

What can you thank God for this morning?

_____

_____

_____

What are important events or people to pray about today?

_____

_____

_____

_____

_____

_____

_____

_____

_____

_____

_____

_____

_____

_____

_____

_____

_____

_____

_____

_____

_____

_____

_____

_____

What sins would you like to confess? What could you have done better?

_____

_____

_____

For what would you like to thank God? What would you like to remember from today?

_____

_____

_____

*"He that hath slight thoughts of sin never had
great thoughts of God."*

—JOHN OWEN

DATE ____/____/____ TODAY'S BIBLE PASSAGE: _____

Reflections on the passage and prayer time

_____

_____

_____

_____

_____

_____

_____

_____

_____

_____

_____

_____

Time in worship ☐   *Time circling prayers* ☐   *Time in listening prayer* ☐

What can you thank God for this morning?

_____

_____

What are important events or people to pray about today?

_____

_____

_____

_____
_____
_____
_____
_____
_____
_____
_____
_____
_____
_____
_____
_____
_____
_____
_____
_____
_____
_____

What sins would you like to confess? What could you have done better?

_____
_____
_____

For what would you like to thank God? What would you like to remember from today?

_____
_____
_____

"Satan loves to fish in the troubled waters of a discontented heart."
—THOMAS WATSON

DATE ____/____/____   TODAY'S BIBLE PASSAGE: _____

Reflections on the passage and prayer time

_____
_____
_____
_____
_____
_____
_____
_____
_____
_____
_____
_____
_____

Time in worship ☐   *Time circling prayers* ☐   *Time in listening prayer* ☐

What can you thank God for this morning?

_____
_____
_____

What are important events or people to pray about today?

_____
_____
_____

_____

_____

_____

_____

_____

_____

_____

_____

_____

_____

_____

_____

_____

_____

_____

_____

_____

_____

_____

_____

What sins would you like to confess? What could you have done better?

_____

_____

_____

For what would you like to thank God? What would you like to remember from today?

_____

_____

_____

"If you want to be popular, preach happiness.
If you want to be unpopular, preach holiness."

—LEONARD RAVENHILL

DATE ____/____/____   TODAY'S BIBLE PASSAGE: _____

Reflections on the passage and prayer time

_____

_____

_____

_____

_____

_____

_____

_____

_____

_____

_____

_____

_____

Time in worship ☐   *Time circling prayers* ☐   *Time in listening prayer* ☐

What can you thank God for this morning?

_____

_____

_____

What are important events or people to pray about today?

_____

_____

_____

_____
_____
_____
_____
_____
_____
_____
_____
_____
_____
_____
_____
_____
_____
_____
_____
_____
_____
_____
_____
_____

What sins would you like to confess? What could you have done better?

_____
_____
_____

For what would you like to thank God? What would you like to remember from today?

_____
_____
_____

> *"Faith sees the invisible, believes the unbelievable,*
> *and receives the impossible."*
>
> —CORRIE TEN BOOM

DATE ____/____/____   TODAY'S BIBLE PASSAGE: _____

Reflections on the passage and prayer time

_____

_____

_____

_____

_____

_____

_____

_____

_____

_____

_____

_____

_____

_____

Time in worship ☐   *Time circling prayers* ☐   *Time in listening prayer* ☐

What can you thank God for this morning?

_____

_____

_____

What are important events or people to pray about today?

_____

_____

_____

_____

_____

_____

_____

_____

_____

_____

_____

_____

_____

_____

_____

_____

_____

_____

_____

_____

_____

_____

What sins would you like to confess? What could you have done better?

_____

_____

_____

For what would you like to thank God? What would you like to remember from today?

_____

_____

_____

> *"Remember that the rule of the kingdom is,*
> *'According to your faith be it unto you.'"*
>
> —CHARLES SPURGEON

DATE ____/____/____   TODAY'S BIBLE PASSAGE: _____

Reflections on the passage and prayer time

_____

_____

_____

_____

_____

_____

_____

_____

_____

_____

_____

Time in worship ☐   *Time circling prayers* ☐   *Time in listening prayer* ☐

What can you thank God for this morning?

_____

_____

What are important events or people to pray about today?

_____

_____

_____

_____

_____

_____

_____

_____

_____

_____

_____

_____

_____

_____

_____

_____

_____

_____

_____

_____

_____

_____

_____

What sins would you like to confess? What could you have done better?

_____

_____

_____

For what would you like to thank God? What would you like to remember from today?

_____

_____

_____

"A true disciple inquires not whether a fact is agreeable to his own reason. His pride has yielded to the divine testimony."

—ADONIRAM JUDSON

DATE ____/____/____   TODAY'S BIBLE PASSAGE: _____

Reflections on the passage and prayer time

_____

_____

_____

_____

_____

_____

_____

_____

_____

_____

_____

_____

_____

Time in worship ☐   *Time circling prayers* ☐   *Time in listening prayer* ☐

What can you thank God for this morning?

_____

_____

_____

What are important events or people to pray about today?

_____

_____

_____

_____
_____
_____
_____
_____
_____
_____
_____
_____
_____
_____
_____
_____
_____
_____
_____
_____
_____
_____
_____

What sins would you like to confess? What could you have done better?

_____
_____
_____

For what would you like to thank God? What would you like to remember from today?

_____
_____
_____

> *"Depend on it. God's work done in God's way will*
> *never lack God's supply."*
> —HUDSON TAYLOR

DATE ____/____/____   TODAY'S BIBLE PASSAGE: _____

Reflections on the passage and prayer time

_____

_____

_____

_____

_____

_____

_____

_____

_____

_____

_____

_____

_____

_____

Time in worship ☐   *Time circling prayers* ☐   *Time in listening prayer* ☐

What can you thank God for this morning?

_____

_____

_____

What are important events or people to pray about today?

_____

_____

_____

_____
_____
_____
_____
_____
_____
_____
_____
_____
_____
_____
_____
_____
_____
_____
_____
_____
_____
_____
_____

What sins would you like to confess? What could you have done better?

_____
_____
_____

For what would you like to thank God? What would you like to remember from today?

_____
_____
_____

"If we do not abide in prayer, we will abide in temptation."
—JOHN OWEN

DATE ____/____/____　TODAY'S BIBLE PASSAGE: _____

Reflections on the passage and prayer time

_____

_____

_____

_____

_____

_____

_____

_____

_____

_____

_____

_____

Time in worship ☐　　*Time circling prayers* ☐　　*Time in listening prayer* ☐

What can you thank God for this morning?

_____

_____

_____

What are important events or people to pray about today?

_____

_____

_____

_____
_____
_____
_____
_____
_____
_____
_____
_____
_____
_____
_____
_____
_____
_____
_____
_____
_____
_____
_____
_____

What sins would you like to confess? What could you have done better?

_____
_____
_____

For what would you like to thank God? What would you like to remember from today?

_____
_____
_____

"The Lord gets His best soldiers out of the highlands of affliction."
—CHARLES SPURGEON

DATE ____/____/____   TODAY'S BIBLE PASSAGE: _____

Reflections on the passage and prayer time

_____

_____

_____

_____

_____

_____

_____

_____

_____

_____

_____

_____

_____

Time in worship ☐   *Time circling prayers* ☐   *Time in listening prayer* ☐

What can you thank God for this morning?

_____

_____

_____

What are important events or people to pray about today?

_____

_____

_____

_____

_____

_____

_____

_____

_____

_____

_____

_____

_____

_____

_____

_____

_____

_____

_____

_____

_____

_____

_____

What sins would you like to confess? What could you have done better?

_____

_____

_____

For what would you like to thank God? What would you like to remember from today?

_____

_____

_____

"If weak in prayer, we are weak everywhere."
—LEONARD RAVENHILL

DATE ____/____/____ TODAY'S BIBLE PASSAGE: _____

Reflections on the passage and prayer time

_____

_____

_____

_____

_____

_____

_____

_____

_____

_____

_____

_____

_____

Time in worship ☐   *Time circling prayers* ☐   *Time in listening prayer* ☐

What can you thank God for this morning?

_____

_____

_____

What are important events or people to pray about today?

_____

_____

_____

What sins would you like to confess? What could you have done better?

For what would you like to thank God? What would you like to remember from today?

"Go to church once a week and nobody pays attention. Worship God seven days a week and you become strange!"

—A. W. TOZER

DATE ____/____/____ TODAY'S BIBLE PASSAGE: _____

Reflections on the passage and prayer time

_____

_____

_____

_____

_____

_____

_____

_____

_____

_____

_____

_____

_____

Time in worship ☐ *Time circling prayers* ☐ *Time in listening prayer* ☐

What can you thank God for this morning?

_____

_____

_____

What are important events or people to pray about today?

_____

_____

_____

_____

_____

_____

_____

_____

_____

_____

_____

_____

_____

_____

_____

_____

_____

_____

_____

_____

_____

_____

_____

_____

What sins would you like to confess? What could you have done better?

_____

_____

_____

For what would you like to thank God? What would you like to remember from today?

_____

_____

_____

"God does not rob our joy, He redefines it. He gives us a deeper, fuller joy when our pleasure is rooted in Him."

—JOHN PERRITT

DATE ____/____/____   TODAY'S BIBLE PASSAGE: _____

Reflections on the passage and prayer time

_____

_____

_____

_____

_____

_____

_____

_____

_____

_____

_____

_____

Time in worship ☐   *Time circling prayers* ☐   *Time in listening prayer* ☐

What can you thank God for this morning?

_____

_____

_____

What are important events or people to pray about today?

_____

_____

_____

_____

_____

_____

_____

_____

_____

_____

_____

_____

_____

_____

_____

_____

_____

_____

_____

_____

_____

_____

_____

_____

What sins would you like to confess? What could you have done better?

_____

_____

_____

For what would you like to thank God? What would you like to remember from today?

_____

_____

_____

"Men do not reject the Bible because it contradicts itself,
but because it contradicts them."

—E. Paul Hovey

DATE ____/____/____   TODAY'S BIBLE PASSAGE: _____

Reflections on the passage and prayer time

_____
_____
_____
_____
_____
_____
_____
_____
_____
_____
_____
_____
_____

Time in worship ☐   *Time circling prayers* ☐   *Time in listening prayer* ☐

What can you thank God for this morning?

_____
_____
_____

What are important events or people to pray about today?

_____
_____
_____

_____

_____

_____

_____

_____

_____

_____

_____

_____

_____

_____

_____

_____

_____

_____

_____

_____

_____

What sins would you like to confess? What could you have done better?

_____

_____

_____

For what would you like to thank God? What would you like to remember from today?

_____

_____

_____

"Prayer is the slender nerve that moves the muscles of omnipotence."
—CHARLES SPURGEON

DATE ____/____/____   TODAY'S BIBLE PASSAGE: _____

Reflections on the passage and prayer time

_____

_____

_____

_____

_____

_____

_____

_____

_____

_____

_____

_____

_____

Time in worship ☐   *Time circling prayers* ☐   *Time in listening prayer* ☐

What can you thank God for this morning?

_____

_____

_____

What are important events or people to pray about today?

_____

_____

_____

_____

_____

_____

_____

_____

_____

_____

_____

_____

_____

_____

_____

_____

_____

_____

_____

_____

_____

_____

_____

What sins would you like to confess? What could you have done better?

_____

_____

_____

For what would you like to thank God? What would you like to remember from today?

_____

_____

_____

*"The beginning of anxiety is the end of faith,
and the beginning of true faith is the end of anxiety."*
—GEORGE MULLER

DATE ____/____/____   TODAY'S BIBLE PASSAGE: _____

Reflections on the passage and prayer time

_____

_____

_____

_____

_____

_____

_____

_____

_____

_____

_____

_____

Time in worship ☐   *Time circling prayers* ☐   *Time in listening prayer* ☐

What can you thank God for this morning?

_____

_____

_____

What are important events or people to pray about today?

_____

_____

_____

What sins would you like to confess? What could you have done better?

For what would you like to thank God? What would you like to remember from today?

"If the devil can't make you bad, he'll make you busy."

—UNKNOWN

DATE ____/____/____   TODAY'S BIBLE PASSAGE: _____

Reflections on the passage and prayer time

_____

_____

_____

_____

_____

_____

_____

_____

_____

_____

_____

_____

_____

Time in worship ☐   *Time circling prayers* ☐   *Time in listening prayer* ☐

What can you thank God for this morning?

_____

_____

_____

What are important events or people to pray about today?

_____

_____

_____

_____

_____

_____

_____

_____

_____

_____

_____

_____

_____

_____

_____

_____

_____

_____

_____

_____

_____

_____

_____

_____

What sins would you like to confess? What could you have done better?

_____

_____

_____

For what would you like to thank God? What would you like to remember from today?

_____

_____

_____

> *"The hour is coming when we shall be astonished to think what mere trifles were once capable of discouraging us."*
> —JOHN NEWTON

DATE ____/____/____ TODAY'S BIBLE PASSAGE: _____

Reflections on the passage and prayer time

_____

_____

_____

_____

_____

_____

_____

_____

_____

_____

_____

Time in worship ☐   *Time circling prayers* ☐   *Time in listening prayer* ☐

What can you thank God for this morning?

_____

_____

_____

What are important events or people to pray about today?

_____

_____

_____

_____

_____

_____

_____

_____

_____

_____

_____

_____

_____

_____

_____

_____

_____

_____

_____

_____

_____

_____

_____

_____

What sins would you like to confess? What could you have done better?

_____

_____

_____

For what would you like to thank God? What would you like to remember from today?

_____

_____

_____

*"If you [only] believe what you like in the Bible,
you don't believe in the Bible, you believe in yourself."*

—MAL McSWAIN

DATE ____/____/____ TODAY'S BIBLE PASSAGE: _____

Reflections on the passage and prayer time

_____

_____

_____

_____

_____

_____

_____

_____

_____

_____

_____

_____

Time in worship ☐   *Time circling prayers* ☐   *Time in listening prayer* ☐

What can you thank God for this morning?

_____

_____

_____

What are important events or people to pray about today?

_____

_____

_____

_____

_____

_____

_____

_____

_____

_____

_____

_____

_____

_____

_____

_____

_____

_____

_____

_____

_____

_____

_____

What sins would you like to confess? What could you have done better?

_____

_____

_____

For what would you like to thank God? What would you like to remember from today?

_____

_____

_____

> *"Let me beg you, not to rest contented with the commonplace religion that is now so prevalent."*
>
> —ADONIRAM JUDSON

DATE ____/____/____   TODAY'S BIBLE PASSAGE: _____

Reflections on the passage and prayer time

_____

_____

_____

_____

_____

_____

_____

_____

_____

_____

_____

_____

_____

Time in worship ☐   *Time circling prayers* ☐   *Time in listening prayer* ☐

What can you thank God for this morning?

_____

_____

_____

What are important events or people to pray about today?

_____

_____

_____

_____

_____

_____

_____

_____

_____

_____

_____

_____

_____

_____

_____

_____

_____

_____

_____

_____

_____

_____

_____

_____

What sins would you like to confess? What could you have done better?

_____

_____

_____

For what would you like to thank God? What would you like to remember from today?

_____

_____

_____

Reminder

There are just two weeks left in this journal!

Remember to order your next one today.

"The [Great Commission] doesn't come with a quota, but with a clarification: teaching them to obey everything I commanded."

—JOHN DICKERSON

DATE ____/____/____   TODAY'S BIBLE PASSAGE: _____

Reflections on the passage and prayer time

_____
_____
_____
_____
_____
_____
_____
_____
_____
_____
_____
_____
_____
_____

Time in worship ☐   *Time circling prayers* ☐   *Time in listening prayer* ☐

What can you thank God for this morning?

_____
_____
_____

What are important events or people to pray about today?

_____
_____
_____

_____

_____

_____

_____

_____

_____

_____

_____

_____

_____

_____

_____

_____

_____

_____

_____

_____

_____

_____

_____

What sins would you like to confess? What could you have done better?

_____

_____

_____

For what would you like to thank God? What would you like to remember from today?

_____

_____

_____

> *"The tyrant dies and his rule is over,*
> *the martyr dies and his rule begins."*
>
> —SOREN KIERKEGAARD

DATE ____/____/____ TODAY'S BIBLE PASSAGE: _____

Reflections on the passage and prayer time

_____

_____

_____

_____

_____

_____

_____

_____

_____

_____

_____

_____

_____

Time in worship ☐   *Time circling prayers* ☐   *Time in listening prayer* ☐

What can you thank God for this morning?

_____

_____

_____

What are important events or people to pray about today?

_____

_____

_____

_____

_____

_____

_____

_____

_____

_____

_____

_____

_____

_____

_____

_____

_____

_____

_____

_____

_____

_____

_____

What sins would you like to confess? What could you have done better?

_____

_____

_____

For what would you like to thank God? What would you like to remember from today?

_____

_____

_____

*"Anxiety does not empty tomorrow of its sorrows,
but only empties today of its strength."*

—CHARLES SPURGEON

DATE ____/____/____   TODAY'S BIBLE PASSAGE: _____

Reflections on the passage and prayer time

_____

_____

_____

_____

_____

_____

_____

_____

_____

_____

_____

_____

Time in worship ☐   *Time circling prayers* ☐   *Time in listening prayer* ☐

What can you thank God for this morning?

_____

_____

_____

What are important events or people to pray about today?

_____

_____

_____

_____

_____

_____

_____

_____

_____

_____

_____

_____

_____

_____

_____

_____

_____

_____

_____

_____

_____

_____

_____

_____

What sins would you like to confess? What could you have done better?

_____

_____

_____

For what would you like to thank God? What would you like to remember from today?

_____

_____

_____

"The secret of praying is praying in secret."
—LEONARD RAVENHILL

DATE ____/____/____   TODAY'S BIBLE PASSAGE: _____

Reflections on the passage and prayer time

_____

_____

_____

_____

_____

_____

_____

_____

_____

_____

_____

_____

Time in worship ☐   *Time circling prayers* ☐   *Time in listening prayer* ☐

What can you thank God for this morning?

_____

_____

_____

What are important events or people to pray about today?

_____

_____

_____

_____
_____
_____
_____
_____
_____
_____
_____
_____
_____
_____
_____
_____
_____
_____
_____
_____
_____
_____
_____

What sins would you like to confess? What could you have done better?

_____
_____
_____

For what would you like to thank God? What would you like to remember from today?

_____
_____
_____

> *"He who runs from God in the morning will scarcely find Him the rest of the day."*
>
> —JOHN BUNYAN

DATE ____/____/____   TODAY'S BIBLE PASSAGE: _____

Reflections on the passage and prayer time

_____

_____

_____

_____

_____

_____

_____

_____

_____

_____

_____

_____

_____

Time in worship ☐   *Time circling prayers* ☐   *Time in listening prayer* ☐

What can you thank God for this morning?

_____

_____

_____

What are important events or people to pray about today?

_____

_____

_____

What sins would you like to confess? What could you have done better?

For what would you like to thank God? What would you like to remember from today?

"The vigor of our spiritual life will be in exact proportion to the place held by the Bible in our life and thoughts."

—GEORGE MULLER

DATE ____/____/____ TODAY'S BIBLE PASSAGE: _____

Reflections on the passage and prayer time

_____

_____

_____

_____

_____

_____

_____

_____

_____

_____

_____

_____

Time in worship ☐   *Time circling prayers* ☐   *Time in listening prayer* ☐

What can you thank God for this morning?

_____

_____

_____

What are important events or people to pray about today?

_____

_____

_____

_____

_____

_____

_____

_____

_____

_____

_____

_____

_____

_____

_____

_____

_____

_____

_____

_____

_____

_____

_____

What sins would you like to confess? What could you have done better?

_____

_____

_____

For what would you like to thank God? What would you like to remember from today?

_____

_____

_____

"Self-pity is ... a sinkhole from which no rescuing hand can drag you because you have chosen to sink."

—ELISABETH ELLIOT

DATE ____/____/____   TODAY'S BIBLE PASSAGE: _____

Reflections on the passage and prayer time

_____

_____

_____

_____

_____

_____

_____

_____

_____

_____

_____

_____

_____

Time in worship ☐   *Time circling prayers* ☐   *Time in listening prayer* ☐

What can you thank God for this morning?

_____

_____

_____

What are important events or people to pray about today?

_____

_____

_____

_____

_____

_____

_____

_____

_____

_____

_____

_____

_____

_____

_____

_____

_____

_____

_____

_____

_____

_____

_____

_____

What sins would you like to confess? What could you have done better?

_____

_____

_____

For what would you like to thank God? What would you like to remember from today?

_____

_____

_____

"The greatest benefactor this age could have is the man who will bring the preachers and the church back to prayer."

—E.M. BOUNDS

DATE ____/____/____   TODAY'S BIBLE PASSAGE: _____

Reflections on the passage and prayer time

_____

_____

_____

_____

_____

_____

_____

_____

_____

_____

_____

_____

_____

Time in worship ☐   *Time circling prayers* ☐   *Time in listening prayer* ☐

What can you thank God for this morning?

_____

_____

_____

What are important events or people to pray about today?

_____

_____

_____

What sins would you like to confess? What could you have done better?

For what would you like to thank God? What would you like to remember from today?

> *"The Church right now has more fashion than passion, is more pathetic than prophetic, is more superficial than supernatural."*
>
> —LEONARD RAVENHILL

DATE ____/____/____ TODAY'S BIBLE PASSAGE: _____

Reflections on the passage and prayer time

_____

_____

_____

_____

_____

_____

_____

_____

_____

_____

_____

_____

_____

Time in worship ☐   *Time circling prayers* ☐   *Time in listening prayer* ☐

What can you thank God for this morning?

_____

_____

_____

What are important events or people to pray about today?

_____

_____

_____

_____

_____

_____

_____

_____

_____

_____

_____

_____

_____

_____

_____

_____

_____

_____

_____

_____

_____

_____

What sins would you like to confess? What could you have done better?

_____

_____

_____

For what would you like to thank God? What would you like to remember from today?

_____

_____

_____

"An ounce of obedience is better than a ton of learning."
—Charles Spurgeon

DATE ____/____/____   TODAY'S BIBLE PASSAGE: _____

Reflections on the passage and prayer time

_____

_____

_____

_____

_____

_____

_____

_____

_____

_____

_____

_____

_____

Time in worship ☐   *Time circling prayers* ☐   *Time in listening prayer* ☐

What can you thank God for this morning?

_____

_____

_____

What are important events or people to pray about today?

_____

_____

_____

_____
_____
_____
_____
_____
_____
_____
_____
_____
_____
_____
_____
_____
_____
_____
_____
_____
_____

What sins would you like to confess? What could you have done better?

_____
_____
_____

For what would you like to thank God? What would you like to remember from today?

_____
_____
_____

"Never be afraid to trust an unknown future to a known God."
—CORRIE TEN BOOM

DATE ____/____/____   TODAY'S BIBLE PASSAGE: _____

Reflections on the passage and prayer time

_____

_____

_____

_____

_____

_____

_____

_____

_____

_____

_____

_____

Time in worship ☐   *Time circling prayers* ☐   *Time in listening prayer* ☐

What can you thank God for this morning?

_____

_____

_____

What are important events or people to pray about today?

_____

_____

_____

_____
_____
_____
_____
_____
_____
_____
_____
_____
_____
_____
_____
_____
_____
_____
_____
_____
_____
_____
_____
_____
_____

What sins would you like to confess? What could you have done better?

_____
_____
_____

For what would you like to thank God? What would you like to remember from today?

_____
_____
_____

"There is no death of sin without the death of Christ."
—JOHN OWEN

DATE ____/____/____   TODAY'S BIBLE PASSAGE: _____

Reflections on the passage and prayer time

_____

_____

_____

_____

_____

_____

_____

_____

_____

_____

_____

_____

_____

Time in worship ☐   *Time circling prayers* ☐   *Time in listening prayer* ☐

What can you thank God for this morning?

_____

_____

_____

What are important events or people to pray about today?

_____

_____

_____

_____
_____
_____
_____
_____
_____
_____
_____
_____
_____
_____
_____
_____
_____
_____
_____
_____
_____
_____
_____

What sins would you like to confess? What could you have done better?

_____
_____
_____

For what would you like to thank God? What would you like to remember from today?

_____
_____
_____

"Prayer will make a man cease from sin, or sin will entice a man to cease from prayer."

—JOHN BUNYAN

DATE ____/____/____ TODAY'S BIBLE PASSAGE: _____

Reflections on the passage and prayer time

_____

_____

_____

_____

_____

_____

_____

_____

_____

_____

_____

_____

Time in worship ☐   *Time circling prayers* ☐   *Time in listening prayer* ☐

What can you thank God for this morning?

_____

_____

_____

What are important events or people to pray about today?

_____

_____

_____

_____

_____

_____

_____

_____

_____

_____

_____

_____

_____

_____

_____

_____

_____

_____

_____

_____

_____

_____

_____

What sins would you like to confess? What could you have done better?

_____

_____

_____

For what would you like to thank God? What would you like to remember from today?

_____

_____

_____

"Only a life of prayer and meditation will render a vessel ready for the Master's use."

—GEORGE MULLER

DATE ____/____/____ TODAY'S BIBLE PASSAGE: _____

Reflections on the passage and prayer time

_____
_____
_____
_____
_____
_____
_____
_____
_____
_____
_____
_____

Time in worship ☐   *Time circling prayers* ☐   *Time in listening prayer* ☐

What can you thank God for this morning?

_____
_____
_____

What are important events or people to pray about today?

_____
_____
_____

_____
_____
_____
_____
_____
_____
_____
_____
_____
_____
_____
_____
_____
_____
_____
_____
_____
_____
_____

What sins would you like to confess? What could you have done better?

_____
_____
_____

For what would you like to thank God? What would you like to remember from today?

_____
_____
_____

NOTES

Printed in the USA
CPSIA information can be obtained
at www.ICGtesting.com
LVHW042336041023
760153LV00014B/38

9 780974 272788